WHAT PEOPLE A

BEING MRS SMITH

The great American mythologist, Joseph Campbell, whose work inspired the *Star Wars* movies, emphasized the importance of the 'hero's journey' of self-discovery and healing. This journey – whether it is physical, psychological or spiritual – means leaving all that is comfortable and socially acceptable in order to encounter giants, dragons and other demons, heal your soul and bring that healing home. In fairy tales, the hero returns in triumph; in real life, the transformation may take a quieter but no less profound form.

Cheryl's lyrical love poem to her husband depicts a true hero's journey. Mr and Mrs Smith took it together at all three levels, each one requiring more bravery than either of them ever thought they might have. They left their home, the conventional path, their consultant, their lifestyle, their country and, hand in hand, embraced the adventure that life was offering them.

She writes of the inevitability of a happy ending; what is certain is that *Being Mrs Smith* is a beautifully-written cocoon of love and happiness within the tempest of crisis. I have been in a similar position and I would have loved to have had Cheryl's book to lead and inspire me to make such a journey myself.
Rev Maggy Whitehouse, author of *The Miracle Man* and *A Woman's Worth*

Being Mrs Smith is an intimate, first-hand account of a couple's healing journey through cancer. It's also a love story. It documents Mr and Mrs Smith's experiences with the healthcare system and their empowerment in moving beyond it to alternative modes of healing, including CBD oil, kambo frog venom, and the vegetal medicine ayahuasca in the Amazon. It offers a raw, honest account of living in the jungle and the politics of the

tribes and the shaman circuit. And it shows, so beautifully, that happy endings aren't as important as happy middles, because love is the thread that binds the whole story together after all.
Rak Razam, writer/producer of *Aya: Awakenings*

There are different ways to face the process which we will all go through when the flesh fails. But each time it happens – and it happens every day – we can either know it or fear it. This is a book that does not skimp on the reality of impermanence, and that is why it should be read. But most of all, because of the love that is and never dies.
Rev Peter Owen-Jones, of BBC documentaries *Extreme Pilgrim* and *Around the World in 80 Faiths*

Being Mrs Smith

A very unorthodox love story

Being
Mrs Smith

A very unorthodox love story

Cheryl Smith

Winchester, UK
Washington, USA

First published by O-Books, 2016
O-Books is an imprint of John Hunt Publishing Ltd., Laurel House, Station Approach,
Alresford, Hants, SO24 9JH, UK
office1@jhpbooks.net
www.johnhuntpublishing.com

For distributor details and how to order please visit the 'Ordering' section on our website.

Cover photograph: Steven Bodzin

ISBN: 978 1 78535 088 7
Library of Congress Control Number: 2015954380

A CIP catalogue record for this book is available from the British Library.

To protect individuals' privacy, all names have been changed, with the exception of Mr Smith.

Design: Stuart Davies

Printed in the USA by Edwards Brothers Malloy

For Mr Smith

Prologue

Monday April 21st 2014
3.45am
Glasgow, Scotland

The taxi driver wants to know whether we're going somewhere nice.

Where we're going is hardly the stuff of small talk. Mr Smith has never been good with small talk anyway, so it looks like it's down to me.

'We're going to Peru.'

'Oh, that's unusual. Holiday, is it?'

'Um, not exactly. We're, uh... going there for, ahmm... medical treatment.'

It's not strictly true of course, but it's close enough and I don't know what else to say.

He changes the subject. His shift patterns are a safer topic of conversation.

Part I
Europe

1

Becoming Mrs Smith

We agreed on a happy ending, no matter what. We agreed that we'd have Ewan McGregor and Kate Winslet in the film version. However, and this is in no way a reflection of my regard or lack of it for Mr McGregor, I can't think of anyone who's anywhere near handsome enough to play my Mr Smith.

Recently I found a photo of him taken at around the time we were first getting to know each other but before we became a couple. What was I thinking? How could I not see immediately that this was the man for me? I mean, it was so obvious. Here was a man of rare beauty. I still don't understand why I didn't pursue him immediately.

But that wasn't how it was. I did see something in Mr Smith that was out of the ordinary. I noted the gentleness, the softness. I couldn't miss it: it was there on his face, open and very inviting. Still, we were a slow burn. It was uncomplicated and companionable, and it was fun. Neither of us was invested in having a relationship – we weren't actively looking. What we found while we weren't looking was treasure beyond expectation.

I think I knew for sure the morning after our first night together, when we shared a shower. The tenderness he showed, the thoroughness with which he washed me, every inch of me, slowly. The deepest part of me knew him then. In later years, his meticulousness and insistence on precision would sometimes give rise to frustration in me, but in that moment I saw who he was, and it's more than possible that I fell in love right there, naked and vulnerable, in the warmth and seclusion of the shower room.

Slow as it was, a few months later he moved in. We'd already experienced the stress of final exams together, followed by a demanding shared summer job. As the only two mature students left standing, having each taken a timeout at different times and for different mature-student reasons, we'd held each other up through enforced sixteen-hour study days and seven-day study weeks. We'd laughed and hugged and wept and shared. We knew who we were for each other, and we were ready.

I remember that time warmly. I was unexpectedly in love with this quiet man with the sometimes wry, sometimes just silly sense of humour, the hilariously foul mouth and the deep, sort-of-greenish-brown eyes. It was never the plan but it was the right thing, and although we couldn't know it then, it happened just when we both needed it to.

There were no fireworks or soaring violins. It was better than that. It was more like the slow alchemy of a fine wine maturing; it was the silent harkening of two souls to their calling to each other. It was the real thing, gentle and sweet and sometimes painful.

I could never understand why he loved me. I asked him to explain and he couldn't. He just loved me, pure and simple. He just did. He just does. He never stopped. Not for one second, and he never will, and therein lies the happy ending that we agreed on.

Life got in the way though, a lot. We were comfortably in love but we had to learn to be happy. We had to learn not to allow life to get in the way so much. It took a while. There were job stresses and money worries and family problems, and then there were health concerns. He was there through it all. He put up with a lot. Some people call that weakness. I call it power. Solid, steady, gentle and deeply masculine strength. It was exactly what I needed to anchor me and keep me safe.

I needed it – needed *him* – in different ways as time passed. We developed a mutual support system in response to our practical and emotional needs, driven by the will to create our happy ending. We didn't ever really have what you'd call a conventional relationship. We didn't do nine-to-five. There were times when I worked to support him through postgraduate study; times when he worked to support me through postgraduate study; times when we worked and played and studied together; times when we barely saw each other; times of disappointment when we had to give up on our plans (when life got in the way)… and then…

I got really sick. Then he lost his job. Then I lost my job because I'd got sick. There were no more job stresses but there were more money worries. I was too sick to take them on. *He* took them on. He was still there. Still solid, still steady, still with me and still willing to do whatever I needed of him. He carried me, a lot of the time literally. His heart hurt. His back must have hurt, when I was so weak that he had to take me upstairs and help me into bed. The touch of his breath on my cheek as he tucked me in, the warmth of him, the faint scent of his essence – I had these to soothe me as I drifted to sleep.

He had no idea whether I would get better, and at times, my condition must have challenged him beyond what was reasonable. One day, he drove me to a hospital appointment and I suggested he take himself to the café with his book rather than face the long wait between consultations. Half an hour later, I found him to tell him what they'd told me – that the vision I'd lost from my left eye couldn't be restored and that I would likely lose the use of my right eye too. It was too much. I cried, right there at the table. He cried too, and he held me. He said he couldn't imagine what such a loss would feel like, but he would feel it with me. What was mine was his, and that included my despair. It was not okay that I was going to be blind. He couldn't make it okay, not even with his magical embrace, but he was there, enduring it with me.

I didn't lose my eyesight though, and under the care of Mr Smith, my health was slowly restored. I'd seen sense, too, by now, and had felt inclined to unsay what I had been saying all along: that I didn't want – no way did I want – to get married again. I'd been there, done that, and it had not ended well. No matter how deeply I felt, I was not going there again. It was messy and unnecessary. Just no. No no no.

That had changed to a yes while I was still on long-term sick leave. I *had* to marry this man. It became imperative at around the time he became my full-time carer and reminded me that the tenderness he'd shown me in the shower those years before was at the core of who he was. It looked like he had no choice but to care for me but, of course, he had. He could have walked away. Just as he could have walked away, when I'd invited him to, after the conversation about children. He would have loved some, and he was still young enough. I'd been through all that already. He'd taken on my teenagers as part of the deal and embraced them as his family, but they were almost adults by the time we met. To choose me had been to give up on something he'd always hoped for, but he'd chosen me anyway.

He'd chosen me again when he'd had no way of knowing whether I'd ever be well again. For a while, it had looked likely I'd be back at work soon, and I'd tried too hard and too fast to get better. That was hard on him because it always led to a crash, and he was the one who was there to pick me up. I broke his heart again and again, but together we always seemed able to mend it.

Resilience was his heart's middle name, and this resilient heart had a lot to teach me. It taught me trust, in the knowing that it would always have my back. It showed me beauty and truth, clearly reflected in the sort-of-greenish-brown eyes. It left me in no doubt of my great fortune in knowing this man and having him choose me. He made me laugh, sometimes by saying or doing something hilarious, and sometimes just from the joy of having him close. It turned out that our elusive happy ending had always been there, weaving a glittering thread through even the roughest parts of the beginning and the middle. We were happy with our daily choices to stay together and to love each other like we'd never loved or been loved before.

He chose all of me, including the not-so-nice parts. He never tried to change me but being around him changed me anyway. That seems to be how true love works. We hold each other and value each other; we give and receive deep respect effortlessly and without judgment; we find a safe place in which to grow. And we listen.

Mr Smith was good at listening, even when I didn't say a thing. Over the years he'd listened carefully enough to hear me change my mind, and when the time came, he'd chosen his moment perfectly. He'd wanted to ask me for years but I'd been so certain I didn't want to, he'd put his own desire aside. He'd waited till I was ready, and if I never had been ready, that would have been okay with him. Whatever I wanted was okay with him. What I wanted was to be Mrs Smith.

The wedding was perfect. When I think of it and look at the photos and the video I'd reluctantly agreed to, the overwhelming impression is green. The ceremony was outdoors in the fullness of summer. I'd chosen a green dress (his favourite colour), and while the river and the waterfall featured heavily (it had rained a *lot* earlier in the day and the river was in gloriously full flood and *noisy*), the trees were luscious and abundant.

So was our mood that day. The sound and picture quality of the video aren't wonderful, but that doesn't matter. When I watch it, I remember exactly how I felt in the moment he turned towards me for the first kiss following the declaration of our vows, and I see not the tiny two-dimensional figures on the screen, but those sort-of-greenish-brown eyes and the depth of what I found there.

There are no words for what I found, and no possible analysis of his commitment to caring for me, which, of course, led to a gradual improvement in my health. I learned how to pace myself and manage my condition, and we defied the doctor's opinion that I'd remain non-functional for life. It's amazing what the right kind of TLC can achieve. It can restore hope and soothe away pain. It can work magic.

It can weave a glittering happy ending out of rough threads. Our story does have a happy ending but it doesn't come at the boy-meets-girl-boy-marries girl, happy-ever-after stage. As is the way with true stories, it's not that neat. This *is* a true story. It's *my version* of the truth, from my memory. Mr Smith might have a different perspective, a slightly different truth, but this is *our* story nonetheless. I know he's happy for me to share it with you and to show you our own flavour of happy ending. But the story comes first, and it starts in the springtime, with the promise of a new beginning.

2

What the Doctor Said

Monday April 16th 2012

We thought it was routine. We didn't know they were looking for what they found.

The money worries would soon be over. Mr Smith had been offered a position in Germany, doing what he'd been doing before our life together began. It wasn't what he *wanted* to do, but the pay was generous, the contract was only for a few years and it would give us the financial security, finally, to put an end to the stress. At the end of those few years, we'd be able to create our happy ending and do what we both *really* wanted to do.

The work itself was easy for him (though it has to be said that Mr Smith has never shirked from hard work), and it would all be virtually stress-free. I was doing much better by now too. I'd even dipped my toe tentatively into some freelance work. I didn't need a full-time carer anymore.

We would miss each other, of course. We'd barely spent a night apart in our eleven-year history. But we knew that in a very real sense we'd be together wherever in the world our respective bodies happened to be. Anyway, he'd come home often, and there would always be phone calls. We agreed that missing each other and then getting together again could add a new dimension to our relationship. The frisson of the airport reunion appealed to us both; the airport goodbyes were worth enduring.

He was doing this for *us* – for our future. Meantime, it would enrich our present. We'd make the most of it, and the most of it was going to add up to a lot. We'd have the freedom to enjoy those reunions in Paris, Rome, Venice… and of course, we'd still be together sometimes at our own hearth in Scotland with our dearly loved dogs and cats in our laps.

It was the promise of this new adventure that brought him to the doctor's surgery, and to that 'routine' appointment that would change everything.

The job demanded stamina. The hours were long, and he wasn't sure he had the energy. He'd been so very tired lately, which wasn't surprising when you considered how full life had been. Taking care of me, the uncertainty of our future, the remnants of past stresses – there had to be consequences.

Those past stresses reached back a long way and we barely noticed their continuing effects. Now it seems clear that they were both a lasting impediment to full health and a catalyst for positive change.

Before we'd come together, he'd had depressive symptoms that had been heavily managed with medication. In our early years, we became aware of their impact only when I asked for his support with a work project. I'd been learning to use a new diagnostic tool to identify issues affecting people's day-to-day lives, and I needed a guinea pig to practise on at home. Of course, he obliged.

On the question 'To what extent do drugs affect your life?', he scored alarmingly highly. For 'drugs', read 'antidepressants', and for 'alarmingly highly', read 'almost off the scale'. Absorbed in my work, family commitments and the weaving of the happy ending, I'd had no idea. Neither had he, until that evening when, committed to helping me with my work assignment, he took the time to sit quietly and really listen to what was going on within himself.

We'd always been health-aware. We ate consciously and we'd both been intermittent meditators for years – when life didn't get in the way. We'd smiled at the popular quote, 'Half an hour's meditation each day is essential, except when you're busy, and then a full hour is required'. We'd groaned in recognition of its truth but now was the time to start taking it seriously. More stillness, more listening, looked a likely first step towards health and freedom.

He took that first step at the local Buddhist centre, where they offered a six-week course in yoga and meditation aimed at increasing mental health. The step turned out to be a leap. Mr Smith was a conscientious learner, and surprisingly quickly, he was no longer on medication. Life became better for us both. He was more alert, more enthusiastic, and generally a happier version of himself. Bolstered by success, we upped our game in terms of diet too. It was never going to hurt, particularly as my own health issues were becoming apparent. We developed an interest in food as therapy and we allowed ourselves some complementary treatments too, when the budget could stand it. A few years later, we would spend part of my pension lump sum on an infrared sauna, a high-powered blender and a powerful juicer, among other things. To become well enough to enjoy the glittering thread in our present and the happy ending in our future, we needed to take better care of ourselves.

It all helped and, over time, we both saw benefits. Still, life happened to us and still we got stressed. We could justify those investments in our health but, nonetheless, we worried almost incessantly about the state of the bank balance, and the juggling of work, study and family took its toll. So far, so normal. So far, so unhealthy, no matter what practical steps we took.

Throughout all of this though, we had each other and we remembered to laugh and love and enjoy life. When the funds were *really* low, we made a game out of challenging ourselves to spend just a wee bit less each week at the budget supermarkets, and to make do with what we had instead of buying new – which seemed a sensible, sustainable and responsible way to live whatever the numbers on the bank statement. We made the best of everything. We were conscious of that glittering thread, still clearly visible among the worried threads, the stressed threads and the why-is-this-happening-to-us threads. We knew what we had: we always, *always* had the softness, strength and safety of loving arms to hold us at night.

Of course, that would change when he went to Germany, but it wasn't going to be forever, and we didn't have to be together in body to be together. Even apart, we were bound by that glittering thread and by knowing who we were for each other.

First though, we had to deal with this tiredness thing, and off he went to the doctor's surgery.

There were no other symptoms. Initial tests showed anaemia, as expected, and iron supplements were duly prescribed. Meantime, more tests were carried out to find the cause: a colonoscopy and gastroscopy, to be performed under sedation at the same appointment. We thought they were ruling things out. We thought it was routine.

While Mr Smith was being attended to in the hospital, I sat in the café downstairs, sipping my camomile tea, reading my book and looking forward to a quiet evening in together. The job was due to begin in early May so there wouldn't be many more of those in the immediate future. When the nurse called to say he was ready to leave, I gathered my things and prepared to take him home.

I wasn't at all concerned to be invited into the consulting room. I understand it's standard practice, when someone has been sedated, to have a loved one present in case the patient is too groggy to remember the conversation once the meds have worn off. Mr Smith looked fine though. He was alert and comfortable, and the softness in the sort-of-greenish-brown eyes said he was looking forward to going home as much as I was. Home, where we'd eat together, maybe with some candles lit. Where we'd linger over the table discussing matters of import and matters of no consequence. Home, where, selfishly, I wanted those eyes to myself, to gaze into and to watch them shine in mirth and in love of life, as they so often did.

We were not expecting the news. The surgeon seemed to think we were. It was as they'd suspected, he said.

It was big. So big and so obstructive that the scope, the diameter of a pencil, couldn't pass through it. They'd had to stop short in both directions, upwards and downwards. His colon had been inflated to facilitate the scope, making it fragile so that any attempt to push the tiny camera through the tumour would have risked a puncture, and that would have meant serious trouble. They would have to operate to be sure of the extent of it, but he *was* in imminent danger. Emergency surgery was required. We were sent home with instructions not to eat anything solid, to pack a bag and to expect a call within forty-eight hours.

He told me later that he'd felt no emotion in that moment, just a sense of calm and the thought, '... so this is what we're dealing with.' He did respond to my squeeze of his hand though. I felt its warm, reassuring pressure as an affirmation that it was all okay. Mr Smith, whose loving care had saved my eyesight and nursed me better, could make it all okay. Of course he could. He always had, hadn't he? He always would, and he always will.

3

What Happened Next

Tuesday April 24th 2012

We always would. We'd learned how to make magical things happen. For me, the magic was always to be found in the sort-of-greenish-brown eyes. For him… Well, I never could figure it out, and he was so often frustrated in the attempt to explain. Then he chose a poem for our wedding ceremony and finally, I heard it:

If questioning would make us wise
No eyes would ever gaze in eyes;
If all our tale were told in speech
No mouths would wander each to each.

Were spirits free from mortal mesh
And love not bound in hearts of flesh
No aching breasts would yearn to meet
And find their ecstasy complete.

For who is there that lives and knows
The secret powers by which he grows?
Were knowledge all, what were our need
To thrill and faint and sweetly bleed?

Then seek not, sweet, the 'If' and 'Why'
I love you now until I die.
For I must love because I live
And life in me is what you give.
Christopher Brennan, 'Because She Would Ask Me Why I Loved Her'

That was what the glittering thread was made of. It had nothing to do with a ticklist of attributes and everything to do with meeting of heart, mind and soul. We could weave it into the dull fabric of the day-to-day to make it shine and into the stretched fabric of the challenging times to make it strong.

Together we could make the dullness of the everyday fabric invisible. Our glitter really was gold – no doubt with a bit of steel too. This magic could deal with anything, which, I'm sure, was why Mr Smith felt so calm that April afternoon.

We didn't get the forty-eight hour call. The surgeon wanted to have her best team available on a day when she could clear her diary completely, and the soonest she could make that happen was just over a week away. We were impressed by her commitment to doing the best job she could, but Mr Smith did seem to be a red-carpet patient, and that felt ominous. While we waited, he lived on soup and smoothies while eyes continued to gaze in eyes, mouths wandered each to each. Then it was time to take him back to the hospital.

We arrived in the ward and immediately the curtains were drawn round the bed. In the time it took for Mr Smith to place his coat on the chair (he had already taken it off so no time wasted) and turn round again, there were eight people inside those curtains. Velocity of gathering. Blow to the gut. This was really happening. It was serious.

I can't identify those eight people when I look back on that day. They were introduced, of course: specialist nurses, anaes-thetists, assistants… their presence was intimidating as much as it was reassuring and I don't remember names or faces. Intimidating had the edge, and it numbed me. What I do remember is how hard it was to leave Mr Smith's bedside that evening.

I don't remember much detail of the following day either. Surgery was scheduled for the morning, I think, and I was to expect a call when it was over. I vaguely recall being advised to stay at home and wait by the phone rather than pace the hospital floor like an expectant father in a vintage comedy. I could see the sense in that – I could be more comfortable at home and I could find distractions (although I do seem to remember sitting on my meditation cushion instead, and focusing *hard*), but I *wanted* to be near him.

They gave me an estimated time for the call. It didn't come. An hour later it still hadn't come. I called them. He was still in surgery. Was that a good thing or a bad thing? My world was polarised. If it wasn't good, it was bad, and I *needed* it to be good.

The 'good' scenario was successful surgery and a complete recovery. That was the only possible outcome in my shattered mind. But the surgery had overrun by more than an hour, and that looked bad. It must have been more complicated, more difficult than they expected – how else could it be taking so long? Maybe he'd died in theatre…

I couldn't dismiss the thought but I couldn't acknowledge it either. I couldn't, just couldn't. No. No, it was good. We were getting the good outcome. They were *really* getting the job done, really thoroughly. That was what was taking the extra time. That was going to heal him; that and the magic thread. It was all okay. The plan was for it all to be okay, always, no matter what.

They called. He was out of theatre and in the high dependency unit. I was welcome to come and sit with him.

I don't remember the drive to the hospital. I don't remember how long it took to find a parking space. I don't remember what I ate that day or what I was wearing. All I remember is the way I felt at the sight of Mr Smith.

He looked wonderful. I don't know how he would have looked to someone who didn't know him, but I imagine they'd have missed that because actually, to the casual observer, he didn't look good at all. The anaesthetic was still in effect and, as I remember, they'd already started him on the morphine. The strong, handsome face had softened and the greenish-brown eyes could hardly focus. Still, he looked wonderful. He looked just like my Mr Smith. In my heart of flesh, my ecstasy was complete.

'Well… it's good to see *you*…'

I had never said anything so true before.

He tried to speak but he needed to rest. There wasn't much strength in his grip when I held his hand, but there was determination in it, not to let go. When the buzzer signalled the end of visiting time, I shifted, reluctantly, tentatively scanning the nurses' faces and hoping to stretch the time just a bit longer. The greenish-brown eyes were misty and wet now. He implored me to stay, and no one asked me to leave.

The surgery had been successful. If you're going to get cancer, the surgeon told him, this is the one to get. The colon has a lot of give in it – like swags in a curtain, she said – and it can stand to lose a few inches. It would take a year or so to adjust to its new position, but she would be keeping an eye on it and all should be well. She'd removed around twenty centimetres, along with some lymph nodes just to be sure, and on analysis, they were confident that they'd got it all. And by the way, the tumour had been stage four.

We didn't know what stage four was, but what did that matter when we had the all-clear? They wanted him to have chemotherapy just to be certain there was no disease still lurking. But he'd done some research during the week of waiting, and he'd asked some questions. He wasn't keen on the potential destruction of healthy cells, or on the possible side effect of permanent numbness in the extremities. His new position in Germany – his livelihood – depended on fine dexterity, and *that* was a sacrifice too far, given that they were telling us there was no cancer anymore. Later, we would sit down with a junior member of the oncology department and pore over the statistics, and they looked encouraging. The facts seemed to support Mr

Smith's intuition: as far as he could see, chemo was both potentially harmful and unnecessary.

Now there was a deep red line running from his ribcage to his pubic bone, and to me, it was precious and lovely. We're not our bodies, of course, but our bodies are part of who and what we are, and as they change, they reflect our being and our becoming. That new marking on his familiar flesh told a story, and as it faded and transformed over the coming months, the new and unknown chapters began to reveal themselves.

The two weeks following the surgery were strangely demanding for us both. For me, every day was Groundhog Day. Get up, shower, walk the dogs, take a call from his sister, make him a fresh green juice (to compensate for the nutritional disaster that is hospital food), shop for whatever he needs today, drive to the hospital, find a space to park, afternoon visit, call his parents from the car or the café, grab a sandwich, evening visit, drive home, take a call from his brother or my daughter or *someone,* tidy up, sleep, repeat… and in any spare moment, research natural approaches to recovery.

We had a head start here. Our interest in natural healthcare had brought us into contact with knowledgeable people and reliable sources. The first person we'd turned to was a friend whose own cancer diagnosis had inspired her to develop natural health conferences and other initiatives. She'd gathered a lot of information and knew lots of impressively qualified and experienced people, as well as patients who had defied terrifying prognoses and achieved complete remission. Sitting at her kitchen table, Mr Smith and I were heartened. There were many stories of recovery, including cases where hope had been relinquished. It didn't look that serious for us. They'd told us his condition was easily operable, so if those people could do it, we could too. We could write our own story and weave healing into our happy ending. We had support from dear friends who believed it too and who knew how to hold us both safe. We were building a team.

We needed them in those two weeks. As I became more exhausted by the moment, Mr Smith's recovery was compromised. One day I arrived for visiting to find his bed empty. He'd been due to transfer to a ward, so I wasn't surprised – until I saw the nurse's face. My gut lurched again. He wasn't in the ward; he was in an isolation room.

4

Reflections and Recovery

April – October 2012

My mind has turned to wondering, since that day, what causes a healthy body to rally such powerful forces against itself.

Mr Smith's passion for community and his longing for unity and harmony were at odds with the society in which he found himself. Concerned by Mammon-worship and the consequent suffering for many, he was exploring ways to reclaim the natural peace that is our birthright, and he devoted his postgraduate efforts to finding alternatives to the capitalist system that he found so abhorrent. Then, in the face of our sudden incapacity to work or study, he was forced to call time on those projects. This naturally affected his emotional state, and the overarching irony of not being able to earn a living only added to the stress.

I have no medical training but I feel and I observe, and I see the impact of the emotions on the physical. Mr Smith's years of near-solitude must have contributed too. His work took him around the world for years and he didn't have much chance to form close friendships till he came to Scotland and finally settled down in one place. In Hong Kong, he contracted legionnaires' disease and almost died. Two weeks in a hospital on the other side of the world, in a dangerous condition and with nothing to do, no one to visit and not even anything to read, will surely have an effect on body, mind and soul.

It was that experience that first brought him to Scotland. It was a wake-up call – life was now demonstrably short and it was time to pursue what he felt was his calling.

The path turned out to be long and broad and very twisted. Since childhood, he'd been fascinated by mystical matters and he'd had some spiritual experiences that had intrigued him. He'd been driven to explore the fullness of human experience, beyond the physical, beyond the psychological. But life had got in the way again till, following the Hong Kong episode and attracted by the parapsychology unit at Edinburgh University, he began to follow his heart. He got himself some entry-level qualifications (which, of course, he excelled in), and he arrived in Scotland at the age of forty.

To his brief disappointment, he never did study parapsychology. Somehow he ended up in the philosophy department, and I'm very glad he did, because I was there too. But in an environment requiring cerebral focus, his intuition was smothered somewhat, a development he bewailed often. 'Had it, lost it,' he would say, referring to his psychic sensibility.

When I became ill years later, I seemed to have the reverse experience: my loss of clarity of thought led to an *increase* in spiritual awareness. The mind took a back seat, allowing my natural wisdom to become more visible. This excited Mr Smith. Later, finally, he would experience it for himself, so much more powerfully, in the Amazonian jungle. He would 'get it back'. He would, in an unexpected way, fulfil that intention with which he first came to Scotland and into my arms.

Meantime though, back in the hospital in 2012, his body continued to suffer. When I couldn't find him in his bed that day, they led me into a tiny room off the high dependency unit. He had an infection, they told me. They were never very clear on what it was, but it delayed his recovery and he couldn't hide the pain. The greenish-brown eyes held no secrets; the handsome jaw was slack and worn. I'd never loved him more.

Eventually, I got to take him home. Sunlight streamed through the large windows of the ward and the grounds outside looked verdant and lush that day. As I helped him pack, the warmth on my face, golden yellow, flowed straight to my heart and it felt like the whole world was conspiring in our favour. He was weak but he was getting stronger. The infection had caused him more pain, more discomfort and more distress than the surgery had, and if my heart hadn't been melted into softness by the greenish-brown eyes, it would surely have shattered at the sight of his suffering. But this was Mr Smith: he was made of tough magic, and he was coming home with me.

Team Smith was gathering strength. It turned out that we knew a surprising number of Reiki masters, aromatherapists, energy healers and generally loving people who were keen to offer us whatever they had: their skills, their time, their knowledge, the loan of a tablet so he could watch DVDs in bed when he had no concentration to read, hampers and healthy homemade treats delivered to our door when I hadn't the heart to shop or cook… It turned out, actually, that people were wonderful.

That, we relied on. We'd made a lot of friends together, *our* friends. We were never one of those gender-split couples, where he goes out with the boys, she goes out with the girls and social connections so often depend on marital status. We were aligned in pretty much everything, so it made sense that we were attracted to the same people. Now, when we needed them, we became beautifully aware of how much community matters; that it's okay to rely on each other.

I'd relied on *him* for the whole time we'd been together, in all sorts of ways and for all sorts of reasons, and I suspect that in some ways, he relied on me too. There had been unacknowledged and unfulfilled needs in both of us – needs we became aware of only when we came together and squeezed love into the gaps to ease out the emptiness. Sometimes it had seemed like the two of us against the world. Often it felt like we needed no one else. We were wrong, of course. People need people, and when we looked up and looked around, we found the *right* people, our team, willing and able to help.

My thoughts return to our wedding poems. In contrast to his earnest and lovely offering, I chose a funny one for him, one that conveyed its message through humour. Its theme was simply my reliance on him. I'd relied on him for a very long time, and now I was going to care for him, with more than a little help from our friends. We were relying on them too now, and they proved as reliable as we knew them to be.

The following months are vague to me now. Of course, he didn't go to Germany. They couldn't keep the position open indefinitely while he recovered, so they gave it to someone else while he was still in hospital. He was disappointed and so was I, but I was relieved too. The money would have solved a lot of problems but there were more important things than money, a truth that had never been more evident.

I do remember being invited to an event taking place the day after he came home. I'd wanted to go but he was much too weak to be left on his own, and anyway, I wanted to stay with him more than I wanted to go out, no matter how exciting the occasion. He'd taken care of so many of my needs for years and I felt it my privilege to be the one caring for him now.

I got a taste of his experiences of previous years, and he got a taste of mine. Of all those times when he'd been frustrated by my attempts to do things for myself when I couldn't. Of all the times when he'd had to stop me, because he knew a crash would lead to more discomfort for me and more work for him. Cooperation in reducing activity was harder than it seemed. Now he was experiencing it for himself – the independent streak that sometimes looked like stubbornness, when all he wanted was to take care of his own basic needs as he'd always done. He apologised. He understood now, and we grew even closer.

At around this time, we learned what a CEA count was. Carcinoembryonic antigens are a marker for colon cancer. This may not be an accurate memory, but we seemed to spend a lot of time in consulting rooms being given numbers relating to his CEA. It was always an encouraging number: there was no cancer.

They'd told us it must have been there for years – maybe as long as a decade – to have grown so big. It wasn't surprising, then, that he felt so much better and was gaining strength so quickly. There'd been a monster lurking within him, at his very core. Growing slowly, it had gone unnoticed, its effects invisible till illuminated by their absence. He'd got on with life anyway, this resilient-hearted man of mine. And very quickly, that familiar, quiet strength became evident in his body as well. With the monster gone, he'd never looked or felt better.

He'd been an athlete in his youth, and now, with his body renewed and strengthened, he wanted to reach for the peak of its potential again. He would train for an Iron Man event over the coming years. The surgeon told him that the five-year survival statistics were low in cases of stage four tumours, and actually, he rather resented that suggestion. The gauntlet was down. In five years, he would either be dead or he would be an Iron Man. There was no doubt over which it was to be.

It wasn't the time for that yet though. With heightened respect for his body, he was allowing it time to heal and rejuvenate. By October he was fitter than any of us, and that's when the call came.

Another position had come up in Germany. Would he be interested in taking it?

5

Moving On

November 2012 – June 2013

It wasn't easy, that first airport goodbye. I wanted to cry but I didn't. This was a positive move. After all the struggles and all the disappointments, life was looking kindly on us. We'd proven ourselves to be invincible and now we had the chance to start again. And we were never apart, not really, so there was no reason to cry. The time for crying had passed.

These were all rational thoughts, but none of them could stop the stinging behind my eyes.

I wanted to sleep, but I didn't. It was just after 6am when I got home and I got out my sewing kit to tackle the hems on his trousers that had needed fixing for months. Sewing wasn't a skill I'd really mastered, but it was something I could do for him for when he got home, and what else was there to do at that time on a dark November morning?

His birthday came just over a week after he left, and I felt bad when I didn't quite get the timing right for his parcel of goodies to arrive. Still, I think we both withstood it well, this first birthday apart. On the phone that night, he reminded me that he'd been used to birthdays alone: he'd had forty-five of them without me. This one had been different to the previous eleven, for sure, but I was still very much a part of it.

We eased into a pattern after a while. We spoke on the phone, of course, on alternate evenings, and there was always a goodnight text. I wrote to him regularly too. I told him he didn't have to reciprocate: he was working long hours and getting to the post office wasn't practical. He'd already had all the news on the phone anyway but he liked to have something to hold in his hands and read, and little notes, cards, poems and the occasional treat from home were always received warmly. I loved writing to him: it helped me feel close to him, even if I didn't say very much. It's a habit I picked up then and have never lost.

Homecomings were special, as we knew they would be, and they were frequent, by necessity, because of the hospital appointments. All routine, and all encouragingly confirming how he actually felt. We couldn't see how it was possible for hearts to grow fonder than ours already were, but the anticipated frisson of reunion did not disappoint. We always made the most of the long weekends and the occasional longer trips home.

Christmas was lovely that year. It was the same as all the previous ones except that the traditions we'd created over the years felt warmer and somehow more meaningful. Mr Smith made more contributions to the Boxing Day family stockings than usual, including the tiny china Santa decorations and unusual novelty chocolates he'd picked up in the traditional German Christmas market. The pay hadn't come through yet so our belts were still squeezed tight, but we did look forward to browsing that market together next year, enjoying Glühwein and Lebkuchen by the harbour. Happy times lay ahead, we were sure.

Happy times did lie ahead, it turned out, but they were to be had in the moment too. The glittering thread was more visible now. If the previous few months had taught us anything at all, they'd taught us to live in the moment and appreciate everything we had. We had a lot, and we'd had it all along. We cherished the moments, even at a distance of a thousand miles. We were still together, just differently together.

Team Smith was still on side. When he was home, we headed to our favourite tea house in town to make the most of their company. When he wasn't, there was the nearby quirky vegan bar where he could eat in the evenings with his colleagues, but the local beers were definitely off the menu. Meantime, we'd invested in a travel blender and I made up our own mix of green powders to send to him so he could make smoothies. Food preparation facilities were limited in his hotel room, but we were still taking good care of him. Each evening, when I urged him to 'look after my Mr Smith', he assured me that he was.

He came home on Valentine's Day, not for the occasion but because we'd booked a weekend of shamanic journeying. His fascination with the ancient wisdom in indigenous healing systems went hand-in-hand with his interest in spirituality, and he'd read a lot on the subject. Together we'd been exploring more directly, and were fortunate to be guided to the best practitioners for us; these were people of integrity and compassion, immersed in traditional teachings. We both found our lives more harmonious and balanced as a result, and we looked forward to the warmth and peace we felt on these occasions.

But it did happen to be Valentine's Day, and while we were never big on red roses or restaurant deals, we never missed an opportunity for an occasion. Not that we needed one – having him home was enough. He delighted me with meaningful little gifts, including the birthday present I thought I'd already had. On my birthday he'd sent me a parcel with a pretty notebook and a tiny Tibetan singing bowl – I'd always wanted a singing bowl – and I was more than happy with those. I didn't know that my real present, the big singing bowl, was still to come. It was the most beautiful singing bowl I'd ever seen. Mr Smith knew how to make a girl happy with his gift-giving, but of course, there was no gift comparable to having and holding him, there in the warmth of our candlelit, womb-like room.

The six-month check had gone well. The wound was often uncomfortable, but Mr Smith wasn't given to complaining and it was hard sometimes for me to tell how he was really feeling. The greenish-brown eyes never lied, that was true, but his health was *so important* to me, I think I convinced myself that he was better than he was. Still, it was temporary discomfort, all par for the course, and on the whole, he did look and feel better. That blood marker was staying down too.

The twelve-month check was late – it can be tricky to coordinate international flight bookings with surgeons' diaries – but eventually, in June, we showed up for the blood tests and the CT scan. The surgeon barely spoke to us; she merely glanced at the scar and pronounced it satisfactory. So far, so good though, and all was well. A few days later I drove him to the airport again.

It was a Wednesday when the call came from the hospital, and he'd only been gone since Sunday. The blood marker was raised and there was something showing on the scan. I was to summon him home immediately for more tests. No time was to be wasted; it had to be right now.

I think I must have gone straight into denial mode. I simply couldn't believe it could be that serious, not when he'd been doing so well. I hesitated to call him, and the positive spin on being in different countries suddenly became hard to maintain. We shouldn't be apart with all this going on. When we're in an emotional kaleidoscope we need each other to cling to as we spin and tumble.

My conscious mind decided that this was just a setback. We'd had lots of those and we would see our way through this one. I called him, he was calm as ever, and I booked him a flight home.

In the hospital room, the surgeon had a question for him: If the colonoscopy showed a recurrence of the disease, would he have chemotherapy this time? Once again, we were staggered by a doctor's casual words.

Stumblingly, he asked how likely that was; she said it was what they expected. He asked whether it would be the same form of chemo that had been on offer last time; she said yes. He said it might mean loss of dexterity in the long term; she said with what we were dealing with here, there may well not be a long term.

There may not be a long term. Or even a medium term. That's

what she said. She also said that she wouldn't arrange a biopsy, and thereby a definitive diagnosis, if he didn't agree to chemotherapy. She needed an answer now. Could we have time to think about it? No, not even five minutes. He turned to me. The greenish-brown eyes. 'What do you think?' All I could say was, 'I'll support you whatever you decide.' He squeezed my hand.

He said yes. We'd researched the effects of chemotherapy. We knew the dangers and we were terrified, but we needed to know for sure whether the cancer was back. We could always change our minds after the biopsy. I was sure he was thinking what I was thinking but there was no opportunity there and then to say so. They took him away and I meandered to that too-familiar hospital café with my thoughts and my fears.

The procedure was described in the nurse's report as 'tortuous', and Mr Smith came round from the sedation to find himself lying on a sweat-drenched pillow. It had been agony for him. His insides were so twisted that they'd needed specialist help to get the scope through.

But, the nurse told us, there was no cancer there. That had to be a good thing, yes? She agreed. So what happens now? They didn't find what they expected to find – what next? She didn't know, but the surgeon would be in touch.

She wasn't. A few days later there was a call asking him to go to the local surgery to have more blood taken, and a week after that came a call from the nurse. To arrange the appointment for the biopsy, she said. He asked what had happened to the promised call from the surgeon to talk things through now that the colonoscopy result was negative. The nurse didn't know what he was talking about.

Strong, resilient, powerful Mr Smith handed the phone over to me, too distracted to hold that conversation any longer. I needed to get clear on what was happening: the biopsy was to be performed if there was disease in the colon, but there wasn't.

They hadn't said it was to be performed *only* if there was disease present though. So they still suspected something? Where was it? Well, the CT scan was showing some spots in the abdomen, so they needed to take a biopsy from there.

Another week passed. The biopsy was performed. Yet another week passed. Life has to go on in these situations. Shopping needs to be done and appointments need to be kept and thankfully, we can't focus all the time on the clouds above our heads. Then, while Mr Smith was waiting in a coffee bar for me to join him after a meeting, the call came.

I found him on a sofa; he stood up to kiss me and give me a little squeeze, and I asked whether he was ready for another cup of tea. Yes, thanks, he was. It wasn't till I'd come back to the table, taken off my coat and performed the usual fussing with cups and trays and pouring from teapots, that he told me what he'd just heard.

The biopsy result was positive. He was to visit the oncologist next week.

6

Turning Point

Wednesday July 3rd 2013

We'd felt battered by the brashness of the surgeon, whose commitment to her patients was tangible but whose open hostility to our interest in natural treatments did little to endear her to us. Her near-violent insistence on an instant decision about the chemotherapy and her general sharpness of tone unnerved us. Too delicate to endure that, we were relieved to move on from her. The oncologist's contrasting softness looked at first like a welcome change, but if you looked deeply enough, there was something disturbing in those big brown eyes.

This wasn't our first meeting with her. A week earlier, Mr Smith had asked her whether there was any natural treatment available and she had said no. Later, through a friend, we learned about mistletoe therapy, available in the campus where she works. The wonderful nurse practitioner who was later to administer it revealed that the oncologist knew of this treatment, its small but potentially significant effect in treating Mr Smith's condition and its ability to alleviate some of the ill effects of chemotherapy. The revelation invoked anger in Mr Smith: why didn't she want him to have treatment that would do no harm and that might do some good? She must have had her reasons, but like her eyes, they were unfathomable to us.

We were less than impressed with the specialist nurse too. We'd found her defensive, aggressive even, in response to what we felt were reasonable questions about the treatments on offer, to the extent that we considered a formal complaint against her. It seemed that some health professionals didn't like to be questioned. Mr Smith and I weren't used to our views not being solicited in matters concerning us, particularly when they concerned us so directly and so intimately. He had read that 'difficult' patients – the ones who ask questions and demand answers – were statistically the ones with the highest recovery rates. We needed sound information on which to base our decisions, and we had no qualms at all, in this case, about being considered difficult. He expressed this sentiment to the doctor, with his customary light humour; the edges of her mouth turned upwards but there was no smile in her eyes.

There was a lot that we didn't know, and over the following months we wished someone would tell us, because much of the time it felt like we were stabbing in the dark. Looking back, I can see that we weren't ready to face the realities that the medics were trying to hint at but never saying explicitly. And in the end, I do see that their reticence allowed us to take advantage of the subjective nature of reality and to reject their story. Frustration was the price of wilful belief, and we paid it, though not exactly willingly.

In the end, we didn't make the complaint. The nurse's attitude didn't sit well with us, but we could see that it came from a real desire to give us what she thought we needed. Anyway, we had enough to occupy us and this was something we could easily let go. I wrote the letter, to release some tension, then I threw it away and we asked for that nurse not to be involved with us again. We agreed that there was something about the doctor that made us uneasy too, but we weren't sure whether that was an intuition we could trust, or whether it was our own fear reflected in her eyes. After all, her job couldn't have been easy; those eyes must have absorbed the sadness of many anguished souls.

Still, we needed straight answers so we asked straight questions. What exactly had they found? What were the proposed treatments? What did she feel about the other, more natural therapies that we were considering?

They'd found some lesions scattered around his abdomen. Most of them were very small; the largest were a few millimetres long. There was a tiny spot on each lung, too small to identify. That didn't sound too worrying to me – not after what we'd already overcome. But this time it was inoperable. The only option was a course of two types of chemotherapy: one in tablet form, the other by intravenous drip once every three weeks.

At home, we'd researched other options: Gerson therapy, liposomal vitamin C, medicinal mushrooms, graviola... we were to use all of these and more over the coming months. The doctor listened patiently but unsympathetically while Mr Smith listed them. Later, discouraged by her lack of interest, we learned not to discuss any of them with her.

Some say you should choose one therapy and stick to it but I suspect those people haven't been told what she told us then, in response to our next question:

'What's the prognosis?'

Those big brown eyes turned away from Mr Smith and met my gaze. I believe she has a husband of her own.

'You have between seventeen months and two years if you accept the chemotherapy. Without it, you have just a few months.'

She carried on talking after that but I didn't hear her. The tears I'd been holding – the airport departure tears, the hospital bedside tears, the solitary night-time tears – now was their time. I clung to Mr Smith and yet again he was strong. He held me, like he always had. Mr Smith, who in that moment reminded me of who he was. Mr Smith, who reminded me of what it was impossible to forget.

I must have believed the doctor in that moment because if I hadn't, the tears would have stayed within me. I'd been very good at holding them in check – an ability I quickly regained – and it took a horror of the ultimate magnitude to release them.

Still there was the incredulity, the inability to believe what she was telling us. It *couldn't* be true. We had *plans*. We had a glittering thread and we were weaving it into our happy ending. It was a labour of love that we needed time to complete. Even as they took him away for yet another blood test, even as the nurse took me into her arms while I sobbed, I began to stop believing in what the doctor had said. We had discussed our mortality on occasion, of course. We knew we would die one day, but we weren't ready to face that day yet. We weren't ready to even think about that day.

I don't really remember going home. Usually I did the driving to and from hospital but I have a vague memory that Mr Smith took over that day. I think we went straight back out to walk the dogs in the woods.

Having dogs to walk was good. It gave us the opportunity to get out among the trees and breathe, and to talk things through in a way that's natural and not forced. There's something about an ambulatory conversation that flows organically and allows us ease to say what we need to say. Being in the woods grounded us and brought us back to the real world – the world where, in the summer, we could pick wild raspberries to feed to each other while we walked. Mr Smith always picked the sweetest and juiciest raspberries to place gently between my lips. The care he took in picking raspberries was a gift to be cherished.

Mr Smith was not afraid of dying, but he had things to do and he wasn't ready to leave. I wasn't ready to let him go and he couldn't bear the thought of me being left on my own. We decided that he was staying.

7

Crisis Point

July – November 2013

We believed it was perfectly possible, despite what the doctor said. We were picking up some solid information about what looked like viable alternatives to drug treatments. The doctor's apparent dismissal of them might have been based on careful review, but to us it seemed more likely that she just didn't want to know. Lacking in expert guidance, we were pulled one way and the other, between pharmaceuticals and the natural health approach.

Both were potentially dangerous, we could see that. We'd read a lot of credible evidence that chemotherapy was harmful and could even be fatal. The doctor used the word 'aggressive'; the disease was aggressive, so the treatment had to be too. A battle to the death, one she expected us to lose. That didn't sit well with Mr Smith, who didn't want a battle, certainly didn't want to lose and could never see the value of aggression in any form. On the other hand, the natural health world was hard to negotiate, with so many claims for miracle cures and so many 'practitioners' and 'doctors' who, on inspection, weren't quite what they claimed to be. People's eagerness to help often led to overload of information about unlikely remedies, and I spent a lot of time deflecting well-intentioned advice with as much grace as I could scrape together.

There was value to be found in alternative methods though, and there was an art in finding the best of them and combining them with conventional medicine in a way that would work for Mr Smith. He made his decision: to opt out of the healthcare system would be to deny himself access to a lot of knowledge and expertise, and he couldn't afford to do that. At the same time, he wanted to do everything he could to keep his body strong enough to withstand the drugs. He needed to be able to relax and be confident in his choices, and a tug-of-war between allopathic and natural medicine didn't appeal at all.

Luckily, he was at least partially equipped to find his way. His research skills, combined with his interest in ancient medicine traditions and a healthy dose of good sense, stood him in good stead over the coming months. He was able to make astute choices about approaches that I'm sure lots of people would dismiss, and to find value in them that might otherwise have been missed. This was becoming less of a battle and more of a quest.

Still we faced what often seemed like battle conditions, with the medics, not the disease, as opponent. As his loyal wingman, I was permitted to stay with him for his first chemotherapy session. First we had a meeting with the pharmacist, to show him our list of natural treatments so he could consult his database to see if anything was contraindicated. If so, he said, Mr Smith would have to discontinue that treatment. He seemed bemused by my desperate response that if something was contraindicated, we would need to decide between that and the chemotherapy. The chemo offered no hope of a cure, while some of these other choices just might. The doctor would not be happy if Mr Smith changed his mind, he said. The doctor, it seemed, was used to having her way.

It turned out that only one substance was potentially problematic. We were to reduce the dose of Reishi mushroom powder, but otherwise there were no issues. It seemed a more than reasonable compromise, and the needle was duly inserted into Mr Smith's arm.

The effects were instant and unpleasant, and they increased over the following week. It seemed wrong that the treatment should reduce him so much and so rapidly when he'd been feeling so well. He lost sensation in his hands and feet, he couldn't concentrate, his vision was blurred, he felt nauseous almost constantly, and at times he had trouble speaking. He couldn't get out of bed for days on end. Meantime, Team Smith rallied again, and we continued with the natural treatments. Gentle yoga helped, as did the regular saunas, but they only went a little way towards alleviating the symptoms.

Meantime, though, the blood marker was going down dramatically. It was hard to attribute this to the chemotherapy alone: the doctor expected it merely to extend his life for a few months rather than to heal him, so the most we'd expected was for the figure to stay the same.

Encouraging as this was, Mr Smith was too distracted by the symptoms to get enthused, and he was beginning to change his mind. During the third cycle, he said he'd rather die now than endure any more. Of course, I treated this statement as hypothetical, but Mr Smith was never inclined to casual comment and his sincerity was clear. A few days later, he almost had his preference met.

On his most recent visit, the doctor had asked him about side effects: was he experiencing any heartburn? He wasn't, but when heartburn-like sensations arose in the following few days, he assumed they were to be expected. They got more severe over time, until one afternoon, on the five-minute walk to post a letter, he barely made it home. He staggered in clutching his chest and fighting for breath. When I called the out-of-hours medical line, they sent an ambulance immediately.

Mr Smith had never had heart problems before but he did now, and it seemed that the angina was caused by one of the chemo drugs. An earnest junior doctor, as yet untrained in what looked to us like a conspiracy of don't-tell, let slip that it could have been fatal if he'd been a few minutes' walk further from home. The senior consultant's attempt at a cover-up came too late, and it took no more than a brief Google search to discover that our oncologist had written a paper a few years before on the potential of one of Mr Smith's prescribed drugs to cause heart failure. This oncologist, when we'd asked her about side effects, hadn't disclosed this to us. It was becoming ever clearer that our allies within the medical profession were few. The quest was not going to be easy with experts once again proving unwilling or unable to share their knowledge with us.

They advised him not to take the pills for the few days between now and his next oncology appointment. They needn't have troubled: by now, he felt that it was the medication and not the disease that was going to kill him, and he'd made a firm decision.

The oncologist suggested that he have the same drug intravenously over three days every week, but he told her he was choosing quality over quantity. He didn't believe in the early death story, but it was the easiest way to communicate his decision, and she accepted it with some grace. Still, the blood marker continued to fall, and his condition began to improve. Shortly after coming off the chemotherapy, we embarked on the mistletoe treatment, which, although it didn't claim to cure, helped him get stronger.

Living in the moment, we cherished peace and renounced everything not conducive to healing. That had to include people: while Team Smith were with us and understood our choices, not everybody did. Mr Smith's well-being took precedence over everything else; we were conscientious about maintaining a hopeful outlook for him, and in some cases, that had to mean letting go.

The acquaintance who invited me to cry on her shoulder and focus on pain and the inevitability of death didn't have her calls returned and was easily consigned to the past. But there were people closer to home whose views were at odds with ours, and those people were trickier to deal with. There was the friend from Mr Smith's earlier life who had recently resurfaced. He took exception when I showed him my feisty side and pointed out in plain language that his drunken 3am calls demanding news were not welcome. Mr Smith, always loyal and making allowances for his friend's own troubles, did resume contact with him later, but I preferred not to. It wasn't so much that I couldn't forgive, it was that I couldn't allow a recurrence. And okay, yes, I was angry: how dare he disturb our nights, our respite from the days?

And there was Mr Smith's sister, heavily invested in his well-being but helpless at a distance of four hundred miles. In need of an emotional fall guy, she held me responsible for decisions that she couldn't support. We both understood that, of course, but the potential for conflict was too high and for a while we sacrificed family unity and retreated to our healing bubble. These tactics were never meant as long-term solutions; we could devote our energies to resolving differences once this was all over, but now wasn't the time.

It was becoming clearer to us that we're all invested, in our own ways, in our stories: the medics who believe so firmly in the paradigms espoused by their professions, and the family members and friends who are pained by our decisions. We were no different: we found our story to invest in, and in doing so, we rejected theirs. Our investment was in getting Mr Smith well, and nothing that got in the way of that had a place in our world.

We preferred to focus on our blessings, which became easier as Team Smith expanded. I was now writing a regular blog about our experiences, and likeminded, knowledgeable people had come forward in response to it. Friends began to introduce us to their friends, and they had things to share. By now, we had a worldwide network of people ready to help with their expertise, their efforts or both. This was a stressful time for us, of course – but there was magic in it too. We weren't facing the horror of imminent death that the doctor told us to expect, because that was too fearsome and we didn't want to live our lives in fear. Encouraged by the sense of community we felt from those who supported us, we believed in life.

Nobody supported us more than the friends who were willing to break the law for us. We'd read a lot about concentrated cannabis oil and its capacity to cure even advanced cancers. Obtaining it and having it at home was risky from a legal point of view, but it might just be worth it. If need be, I was willing to go to prison to bring my Mr Smith back to health, and thankfully, I wasn't alone. I have no idea how they did it, but some members of Team Smith pulled together and had some oil sent to us. It wasn't a full course and it almost ruined us financially, but it was here in our hands and it gave us some hope.

In September, we visited a friend in the south of England to take part in a Kambo circle and to have some sound healing. Kambo, frog venom introduced through the skin, had been the subject of some encouraging and credible research into potential cancer cures. As always, Mr Smith was guided by his particular blend of intuition and good sense, and although he would need a course of treatments, this first one did give him an enhanced feeling of well-being. During this visit we learned more about Amazonian traditional medicine, a subject that had fascinated Mr Smith for years. Our friend had learned the art of shamanic medicine with a *curandero* in Peru, and he felt that a month or so in the jungle might help with healing. Mr Smith had always felt drawn to Peru without really knowing why: maybe this was it. We agreed we would find a way to accompany our friend there at some time in the near future. Meantime, with the cannabis oil, the mistletoe and a lot of love and hope, the blood marker continued to drop.

So far, so encouraging, and what we were encouraged to do was to live gently. Mr Smith had slowed down at last, and I took the role of full-time carer seriously. We were still everything we always had been for each other; nothing could change that. Possibly, there was a touch more tenderness between us, a softening. I had always melted at the sight of Mr Smith, but now, maybe, I melted more. He had always made me laugh a lot, but now, maybe, I fell into his arms just a wee bit more readily when the giggles struck. It was around this time that a new little regular exchange found its way into our vocabulary:

'Do something for me?'

'Uhuh?'

'Don't die…'

'I won't die…'

And the smile appeared again in the greenish-brown eyes, and his arms were safe, and all was well.

Amidst all of this, there was a too, too solid problem that the love and the care couldn't chase away. Mr Smith's earnings from his time in Germany had been spent, and my freelance work had dried up long before. We were having to rely on benefits but through a comedy of errors we fell through loophole after loophole and our income was barely enough to subsist on. To heal, we needed more than that. We needed to *live*. We needed not to have the stress of worrying about whether we could pay the bills. We needed good quality fresh food and we needed treatments, and those didn't come cheap.

Mr Smith had the solution: he would go back to work. The stress was beginning to get to him, and that wasn't going to help him get better. He would rather be working, worry-free and earning enough to pay for a course of Kambo or to go to Peru where there was hope of complete recovery.

Guilt hit me hard. In our dance of who earns when, *I* should be taking the lead and supporting us financially at this time. But I hadn't been in work for more than five years and my skills were sorely out of date. Any attempt to find a job would just add another layer of stress. To start something new would take a while and there were no guarantees. Mr Smith, on the other hand, had a well-paid position waiting for him – and it *was* a stress-free solution in terms of the work itself. He assured me he was feeling strong enough.

It was a year since he'd first left. This time, I insisted that he stay till after his birthday. There were to be no more birthdays apart, ever.

8

Knowing What Matters

November 2013 – January 2014

The café near the departure gate at Glasgow Airport has shallow booths lined with curved benches, where Mr Smith and I used to share our last precious minutes before his early morning flight to Amsterdam and onwards to Hamburg. At 4am it was quiet there and, still warm and sleepy from the bed we'd left behind, we could stay close, discreetly. When the time came for him to go through the gate, we'd wave and blow kisses till he was round the corner and out of sight.

That was a memory now: there was a new service flying directly to Hamburg from Edinburgh, and it cut several hours off his journey. This flight departed later in the day and there were no booths, just separate armchairs and lots of people. It just wasn't possible to get as close as we needed to be in those last few minutes, and that hurt.

That day, the sun was low and unusually bright through the glass walls, and as we walked towards the gate, I became aware of the song that was playing in the background: *Don't Let the Sun Catch You Crying*. I couldn't obey. So many goodbyes had finally taught me that tears are there to be shed, and this time I let them flow. On the way home the radio was relentless. As I pulled out of the car park, *Forever Autumn* filled my ears with its plangent repetition of 'Now you're not here…', and by the time I got home I found myself listening to *Alone Again (Naturally)*. I had to smile and save the story for that evening's phone call.

Later I got back into the car to do some shopping, and now they were playing a selection of Paul Young songs: *Everytime You Go Away* and *Come Back and Stay*. It seemed that someone at that radio station was inside my mind that day. In the coming months, songs became ever more significant: they began to come forward on our behalf, to communicate the depths of our knowing that we didn't dare to speak.

We thought the return to work would mark a calmer phase; we were wrong. A few days after Mr Smith left, I found us the perfect home to move into. Our house had been on the market for some time and, rather than wait for it to sell, we'd decided to give Fate a little nudge and begin the search for somewhere new. People expected us to withdraw from selling when Mr Smith was diagnosed, but it became even more important to move on: we were still living in my old marital home and we craved a fresh start. This rental property was the ideal stepping stone from where we were living to the sustainable, eco-friendly home we planned to build as part of the community that was Mr Smith's passion. A few months later we would sell our house, freeing up a smaller sum than we'd hoped for, but that didn't matter too much, and as it turned out, we wouldn't spend it according to plan anyway.

The old house was never quite right for us but we'd melded our tastes and our skills, and created a haven in it anyway. With his own hands Mr Smith had built a hearth, the symbol of everything he cherished: warmth, light, conversation, music, family, community. He'd pulled down walls, built a staircase and created so much of what was right about that house, and he had done it all to his usual standard of near-perfection. I was a bit sad to leave all this but he said we'd do it all again in our permanent home – the one we were going to create from the ground up; the one we were going to grow old in together.

Meantime, we would fill this temporary home with the artefacts of our story: the furniture we bought together, the crafts we made, the pictures we painted and the gifts we chose for each other. In a few weeks it would feel more like home than the old house did, and we would spend blissful days and nights there. First though, he was coming home for Christmas.

Again, we didn't get to enjoy the German Christmas market, but that didn't matter. On the way to pick him up from the airport, I laughed with joy in anticipation of being with him and of our own special little rituals. As always, we snuggled up to watch *It's a Wonderful Life* (and as always, he wiped away my tears when I cried at the end), and we sipped our mulled wine and ate our homemade mince pies. The gifts were wrapped and under the tree, and our glittering thread was reflected in the flickering of the candle flames. On Boxing Day we found little treasures in our stockings: always a bookmark, always a crystal for him to keep in his pocket, more tiny china Santas and, this time, an angel or two. Of course, these little gifts didn't matter in themselves; what mattered was the loving care that had gone into the choosing of them. We were very clear now about what mattered.

We got the keys to the new house on the first Tuesday of the year, and even with no furniture yet, we planned a combined housewarming and leaving party for Friday evening. As ever, the trip home had been too short and Mr Smith was due back at work on Monday.

This was another week of hospital appointments. On Tuesday the oncologist was concerned about the blood marker: the count from just before Christmas was raised slightly. On Wednesday the cardiologist declared his heart healthy again, with no lasting damage. That sounded like good news until he remarked that the oncologist would be pleased: this would mean that she could resume the chemotherapy. He betrayed an agenda different to ours and, while it was no surprise, it was a blow to the heart. On Thursday there was another CT scan, followed by a visit to the mistletoe nurse, who always made everything feel better. On Friday morning we were back in the oncologist's room.

The word she used was 'worse'. The blood count was raised again and the lesions were bigger. He would have to go back on the chemo. He had already rejected the idea months before, but since dying was not on the agenda (he'd promised), we had to do *something*. He told her he needed time to consider the options.

We almost cancelled our little gathering that evening but we decided not to: looking back, I think we were both in shock and we needed the distraction. I have a group photo taken on that night, where we're all laughing, so Team Smith must have worked their usual magic. Saturday passed quietly, and early on Sunday morning, my airport tears were punctuated by sobs as I drove away alone.

Questions. Why did I let him go back to work? Could I have stopped him? Did I know then what I know now? Did he? If we'd admitted to ourselves what we knew, would things have been different?

But the questions don't matter anymore and, anyway, the answers are clear now. This path was necessary for Mr Smith, the only one he could have taken, given what he knew about traditional medicine, about healing, about the horrors of conventional treatments, about the wisdom in his soul. Still, as a pragmatist, he went back to Germany because we had no other way to earn the money we needed for the next stage of the journey, a vital step in his healing. Our shaman friend was planning a visit to Peru in April, and Mr Smith was hoping to go with him. It had to be this way but guilt and fear mingled in me, and the pain of missing him was harder than ever to endure.

This time round the phone calls were longer and more frequent; we spoke every night. On one of those calls, he told me about a new song he'd heard, one that had touched him so deeply it had made him cry. He had long before distinguished between macho and masculine, and the latter, which he embodied fully, could admit tears. It was a simple song that spoke obliquely of love enduring through the apparent separation of death. I found it online as soon as we said our goodnights, and immediately I understood its effect on him. We did know, both of us, why it held such power, and my conscious mind was very afraid of it. I wanted nothing other than to have my Mr Smith close to me.

The two weeks between his leaving and my joining him for my birthday were full of activity but still they passed slowly. Moving furniture, sorting out years of stuff, packing and making sure I had his mistletoe supplies ready to take to him all seemed too much, and by the time I drove to the airport early that Sunday morning, every part of me was exhausted.

He met me in Hamburg and those two weeks melted away. He looked strong and healthy and the greenish-brown eyes had a sparkle in them that made it hard to believe the oncologist's story that he was dangerously ill. Reunited, we would no doubt discuss what to do about that over the coming days, but meantime, I was reassured.

Finally I got to put faces to names and match scenes with stories. It was a heavenly release, a whole week to spend together doing only what we wanted to do. We planned on travelling beyond his everyday environment but I wanted to see his little part of Germany too. We began with supper in the local vegan bar, chatting to the regulars but mostly holding hands and smiling to each other.

Next day, my birthday, Mr Smith couldn't get out of bed and he couldn't stop apologising. Lethargy had caught up with him and I worried that he was working too hard. When, eventually, he felt well enough, the day was half over but we were content to stroll around the town and find a cosy nook in the bar overlooking the harbour.

On Tuesday he felt better, but at bedtime, what should have been the sound of teeth being brushed was unmistakably the sound of something else. One moment he felt just fine; the next, he was vomiting uncontrollably, and when I got him into bed, he was shaking. Next morning, we were at the local doctor's surgery.

There was no recurrence of the vomiting that week but there was pain, and the doctor ordered tests to find out what was causing it. A hospital appointment was arranged for Monday, the day after I was due to go home. Mr Smith apologised again: this wasn't what we'd planned and he hadn't been able to make my birthday special. I told him it *had* been special because he'd been by my side in every moment, and anyway I couldn't have borne the thought of him being so sick without me there to care for him.

But I had to go home, and now I was the one apologising, for leaving him. Financially and practically, we couldn't find a way for me to stay, and when we had that role-reversal parting on Sunday, it felt that Fate was cruel to separate us.

9

Finding Our Path

February – March 2014

The following weeks are a jumble of worry and hope in my memory now, though I do remember that he was encouraged by the standard of medical care in Germany and the speed with which they got things done. They quickly diagnosed a build-up of fluid in his left kidney, probably caused by a stone. Kidney stones are notoriously painful but they're not in the same category as terminal cancer, and we were relieved – till an ultra-sound scan showed no sign of one.

Still we had hope. More cannabis oil was on its way. The original source had dried up and it had taken a while to find a new one that was reliable and discreet and that would ship to Germany. Our Kambo practitioner was coming to visit us at home in March, and, finally, we were going to Peru.

Our English shaman had changed his plans to visit his *maestro* in April, but he had an alternative that sounded even more promising. He knew someone who had a place for us to stay as long as we needed to, the expertise to support us and the local knowledge to introduce us to genuine and gifted healers. Her home was safe – not in the depths of the jungle where there were health risks – and she could bring the right people there to work with us. She knew the difference between those shamans too ready to take the *gringo* dollar and those with pure lineage and solid working practices. She could protect us from predators and bring us the best. It was a rare opportunity.

Over the next few weeks we would establish contact with this friend of a friend and get very clear on what was involved. She had a team in place to care for us, meeting every need from local transport to domestic comfort to ceremonial healing sessions.

Something within Mr Smith – intuition, or innate wisdom – told him this was right for him. We'd worked with ayahuasca, the most commonly known of the Amazonian plant medicines, in the previous few years, and through those experiences, he'd opened up and learned to listen to that voice.

One evening on the phone, he told me clearly of his intention: 'I'm going to Peru, and I'm going to stay till the job is done.'

I wonder how many people would have made the decision that Mr Smith did, in the circumstances. But nobody else ever has been in his circumstances; they were unique to him, and so were his insights and the sum of the information at his disposal. He knew something about the way the plants worked and about the documented cases of complete remission. More than that, he knew these practices had the potential to open him up to healing on emotional and spiritual levels, regardless of what was happening in his body. This opportunity was here for him, now, exactly when he needed it: of course he was going to take it. And of course, I was going to be right there at his side.

Meantime, the thousand miles between Scotland and Germany felt like light years. The pain of being apart, added to Mr Smith's chronic physical pain and my anguish of helplessness, was impossible to bear now. But we were getting used to bearing the unbearable, and it wouldn't be necessary for much longer. It would be over soon.

In March, my son had guests to stay. He still lived with us but now he was making plans to move to Sweden to be with his partner and her four-year-old. I loved having my boy around, especially while Mr Smith was away, and I'd miss him, but we were happy for him and we were looking forward to finally living alone, just the two of us. Although we'd met my son's partner on several occasions, this was the first visit from this new little family. Mr Smith missed it but he was looking forward to meeting our new almost-grandson, maybe later in the year.

He was coming home for the Kambo circle a week after they were due to leave. By now we'd invested all our hopes for healing in the trip to Peru but this circle had been arranged for a while. We'd taken advice from our practitioner, a knowledgeable and wise woman, and the frog medicine was compatible with the Peruvian plants and very much worth having. We were looking forward to its cleansing effects and to the healing effects of sharing the experience with good friends.

We knew a lot about the power of friendship. The previous summer, we'd gathered some of Team Smith together in our home to meditate and share offerings of healing. We proved to Mr Smith how very deeply and widely loved he was – something I don't think he'd fully grasped before. People from several religious traditions, and people from none, came and offered rituals and tokens, and people who couldn't join us in person sent messages and supported us with distance reiki and other energetic methods. We even had wedding flowers from the previous day on our altar, donated by the bride who broke with tradition and offered her red roses to us rather than throwing them to the single women. It was potent medicine, this nurturing occasion full of laughter, happy tears and hugs, and the memory of it helped sustain us both now.

Our phone calls became more frequent – two or three a day – as Mr Smith got more involved with the doctors in Germany. He was seeing an oncologist over there now, and I was tangled in the red tape involved in the sharing of his medical records, so there was a lot to discuss. As the frequency of his hospital visits increased, his attendance at work decreased in proportion. Uncharacteristically, he was beginning to admit the extent of his pain.

One anxiety-filled Wednesday afternoon, the day before our Swedish family was due to leave, the phone finally rang and he reported on his latest consultation. It wasn't encouraging news:

the blood count was almost double what it had been back in December. The fluid in his kidney wasn't draining and whatever was constricting his ureter had to be dealt with. It might be scar tissue from the surgery or it might be a cancerous growth; they couldn't tell. He had another appointment for Friday.

By now I was used to acting quickly, this time in response to the distress in his voice. I've never known anyone as strong and capable as Mr Smith. Now he was strong and capable enough to be clear about what he needed in this moment of weakness. He needed me with him, and I needed to be there.

An hour later I called him back: I would be with him tomorrow. The relief in his voice flooded my awareness.

I'd bought a one-way ticket: we had no idea what would arise in the immediate future but we did know that we had to be together. All plans were suspended: we resigned ourselves to the possibility of relinquishing his ticket home for the following week and we warned our Kambo circle that the arrangement might have to be called off.

This time he was too weak to meet me at the airport so I made the two-hour bus journey on my own. And there he was, my Mr Smith, waiting at the bus station, familiar and handsome though noticeably different. He looked wearied, but his smile was the same smile and his embrace and his kisses were as warming as ever. My heart did a little flip at the thrill of them, and then it broke for the harm to this body, the body that delivered them with such exquisite tenderness.

On the short walk to the hotel, he suggested stopping at the harbour bar for a glass of wine and a chat. He fancied a little treat for us both. He'd relaxed his dietary rules a little, knowing that being too strict could create more stress than it removed. One drink was permissible on occasion, and as always, this reunion was an occasion. Wanting to stay out and relax with some wine showed the kind of everyday spontaneity that had always flavoured our time together, and it tasted of normality and reassurance.

Settled and snug in the swing chair, we sipped in silence; for a while there was no need for words. Eventually he said he had something to tell me, and my heart lurched once again at the troubled look on his face. Was it bad news? Was it about him? No, no, he said, it was about his dad. Poor Mr Smith Senior: at ninety-one, he was going through health crises of his own to add to his worries about his son. My Mr Smith had this new burden to deal with and of course I was concerned too, or rather I would have been if I'd been able to feel beyond the immediate surge of relief. For now, Mr Smith was okay. It was still possible to believe in his recovery.

10

Messages From Ourselves

March – April 2014

I don't remember much about the doctors' appointments that week, but I do remember that the oncologist wasn't concerned about the blood count. It was raised, yes, but it was still under ten, which he considered very low. That morning he'd seen someone whose count was in the thousands. We had understood it was the trend, not the number, that mattered, and while we were more than willing to accept this new view, it was very different from what we'd been told back in Scotland. Amidst our confusion, it allowed us to reason that one or two heightened readings weren't enough to reverse the downward trend. We could still deal with this.

I do remember the terror. The inevitable lurching moment of panic over whether we'd made the right decision: maybe it was better just to do what the doctor advised? But Mr Smith was certain of his choices, and I trusted him. In any case, there were no more options within the realm of conventional medicine. To go home would be to succumb, not only to an early death, but to poverty and the misery that came with it; to stay in Germany and be admitted to hospital seemed a more comfortable option but it would yield the same result, and anyway it wasn't economically viable. Being there depended on his income and, to add to the stress, he hadn't been paid for weeks.

The German oncologist seemed more positive about the possible outcomes than our doctor in Scotland. He was fascinated by the literature on our chosen treatments, and was happy to monitor Mr Smith as he walked this unorthodox path. In the end we were reassured to finally have the medics on our side.

Meantime, there were the mistletoe injections and the strong painkillers the doctor had prescribed, and we were able to reinstate our plans for Kambo at home. I managed to book a seat on the flight that he was due to take on Thursday, and we settled into the comfort of being together.

I don't remember how many times we visited consulting rooms in that week. The significance in my memory lies much more in the intensity of the strange happenings and the symbols we either cast aside in fear of what they might mean, or could only make sense of with hindsight.

Our errors of rational thought can get in the way of accepting what we know. Too often we dismiss our own wisdom, assuming that if we can't prove it, it doesn't exist. Mr Smith knew that this was a mistake – he was fond of the maxim that absence of proof is not proof of absence – and anyway, for a while now the evidence of our senses hadn't needed proof. There had been quite a few happenings that had stretched our everyday understanding, and of course, our experiences with ayahuasca had shown us that there's more to existence than we can ever measure in the physical. Still, out of fear, we often turned away from what we could have learned.

Music and poetry hold a unique ability to excavate the depths of our knowing, and once again, it was through song that Mr Smith told me what he couldn't say directly. Our earliest days together, studying, eating, sleeping and living intensely in his tiny student room, had been infused with the songs of Leonard Cohen, a man Mr Smith admired and whose words had inspired him countless times. Now, in his tiny hotel room, living with a different but no less powerful intensity, again Mr Cohen filled our heads and hearts with new melodies and new words. Once again, the simplest words had spoken of his deepest experience.

Show me the place where you want your slave to go
Show me the place, I've forgotten, I don't know

Show me the place, for my head is bending low
Show me the place where you want your slave to go
From *Show Me the Place,* written by Leonard Cohen.

These were words that spoke of weariness to a man who'd just about had enough; who'd struggled and who, momentarily, had forgotten why. To a man who, finally, was ready to surrender his suffering and to trust in whatever Fate, or God, or the Universe, had planned for him.

Every song spoke to us now, and the music had messages for us both over the coming months. Meantime, there was something different about the greenish-brown eyes.

They were no longer greenish-brown. On the morning after I arrived, the daylight revealed them to be the colour that the night sky should be but seldom is. I've read that eyes can sometimes change colour with age or disease, and that this happens through loss of pigment. This looked like something different: there was still plenty of colour in those depths.

'Wow, look at you! Your eyes have changed.'

'Have they?'

'Yes! They're *blue!*'

'Well, I wonder what that means?'

And he smiled and the deep, dark blue eyes shone.

They carried on shining. Over time, they became still brighter, clearer, deeper. Despite the worry, despite the stress, in the midst of uncertainty, it was impossible to look into those eyes and not be assured that everything was okay.

That Sunday afternoon, I knew for certain that everything was, and always would be, okay. It was both the most wonderful and the most terrifying experience of my life so far.

Mr Smith had bought a piece of cannabis resin from someone at work. Assured that it would provide a natural respite from the pain that was now a constant and draining presence despite the medication, he was willing to bend the law slightly for the sake of some release. We'd never taken anything like this before and he wanted us to do it together. As always, I was happy to support him, to share this experience as we'd shared so many others. I'd been assured that in a low dose, it would have a relaxing effect, and that certainly wasn't going to hurt.

We got the dosage wrong. What was a two-person dose to the supplier, a veteran user of some decades, turned out to be more of a ten-person dose to beginners like us, and its effect was intense. We both fell asleep almost immediately, and when we woke we thought it was all over.

That was when I began to be really scared. I descended to a very dark place, repeatedly, over what felt like a lifetime. Mr Smith held me close – I couldn't be parted from him for even a moment – and between the times of terror, there were moments of exquisite beauty. I felt his love amplified; I experienced his gentle words as balm for my soul. I knew it intimately, this heightened sensation that I'd never felt before in this life. Then I plummeted to the dark place, and I begged him to save me from it. I didn't know what it was but I couldn't go back there. I *had* to stay awake.

At last it was over, though it took some days for me to be able to grasp a conversation properly again. Mr Smith said that he'd felt himself entering an altered state but he'd snapped back to this reality when he saw that I needed him. He'd had respite from the pain though, for a while. He'd been wanting to ask me something.

'What was it that you saw, before you got scared?'

'I'm not sure...'

'Well, whatever it was, it was wonderful. You had an expression of utter joy and you were gesturing, "Wow, is this really for me?" You were looking up into the corner of the room and I don't know what you saw but I've never seen anyone look like that before.'

Then I remembered, in clear and fine detail. The medicine

helped me open up enough to see something not of this world. Since that moment when Mr Smith reminded me, I haven't forgotten it again.

What I saw was Mr Smith, in a form that language can't describe. The closest I can get is to say that he was made of light, yet he was more himself, more real, than I'd ever seen him before. He was radiant, beautiful, perfect, and he was smiling at me in a show of purity and unbounded love. Everything was okay. Everything was so very much more than okay, and it always would be.

Then I got scared, and I went to the dark place. I didn't know then where the dark place was, but now, I think I do. The dark place was my fear – fear that to be the radiant version of himself, he would have to relinquish the physical version. And the fear was every bit as real as the Mr Smith that was made of light.

On Thursday we went home, together for once. On the long, late evening drive from the airport, he called his parents' home. Mr Smith Senior had been due to have a limb amputated that day and we'd never known him so dispirited. Mr Smith had expected his brother to answer the phone, and he let out a little cry of surprise and delight at the sound of his dad's voice. He'd been given a last-minute reprieve when a senior surgeon had vetoed the decision. Things were beginning to look brighter for the Smiths.

It was late and we were exhausted when we got home, but I was too excited to wait till morning. Mr Smith had bought me a course of pottery classes as my birthday gift, and I'd used it to make him a Green Man plaque. I'd given him a carved wooden one for Christmas and, though he'd loved it, he'd mentioned that he'd like to have a more traditional one too someday. That was why I'd asked for the pottery course. He loved his welcome home gift. He loved it even more when he realised I'd made it myself, and when I told him I'd pressed the leaves from the oak tree that he'd always felt was 'his', he was overcome with appreciation. That, for us, was the joy and the art of gift-giving. We slept soundly that night, he in the simple contentment of knowing that someone loved him enough to make a Green Man for him.

The Kambo sessions were intense and challenging for us all, but especially for Mr Smith. The rest of us had one session; he had three, and I lost count of the total number of points burned on his skin for the medicine to enter. The effect was immediate. Kambo always induces vomiting, composed mostly of the water we need to ingest in large quantities beforehand, but Mr Smith was releasing a lot of fluids too unpleasant to describe. He was doing heroically, the practitioner told us, and it made sense to us that these substances needed to be purged. He was so weak that for a long time he lay shivering on the bedroom floor despite being wrapped in several blankets and a duvet, with me holding him close for comfort and warmth. It was hard, very hard, but worth it. He felt a shift, as if something big had been dislodged. The benefits showed themselves over the coming days and the experience left him strengthened for what lay ahead.

We continued our communication with the contact in Peru. Our many questions were answered and we were given practical advice to prepare us for the journey. We booked our flights and planned to stay for a month.

Mr Smith went back to Germany stronger and more able to cope, while life at home was filled with activity. Our house was sold and had to be emptied and cleaned – quite a feat when the attic was packed full of boxes of books and tools of every description that Mr Smith hadn't had the time or the stamina to sort through. It was a timely development though, as it would free up some funds for the treatments in Peru. The plans to put the money towards our new home were on indefinite hold now our priorities had changed.

Our host had assured us that she herself wasn't interested in money. She was approaching the end of a four-year apprenticeship in *curanderismo,* the art of shamanic healing, and Mr Smith's case would give her an opportunity to practise under the close supervision of one of the most respected *curanderos* in the country. We would be paying far less than the typical tourist rates; still, the money from the house sale was a useful addition to the modest budget we'd managed to put aside.

Once again, Team Smith was on hand. A friend agreed to take care of our new home and our pets while we were away. We needed her: my son had just announced that he was moving to Sweden the week after we were due to leave. Finally, the empty nest. We would need a housesitter for longer than we'd thought, too: our host in Peru was concerned that we planned to stay for only a month. It would take longer than that, she said – three months at least. There must have been a misunderstanding, probably because our shaman friend's original plan had been for a month. Our return tickets were non-refundable, but by now we didn't care: we were on our way.

Mr Smith finally came home on the 9th of April, and this time it was for good. We'd decided that he wouldn't go back to Germany: if we'd learned anything these last two years we'd learned that living together was more important than any sum of money; that life was about loving and not about striving; that we were going to trust that we'd get what we needed to thrive without the stress of separation. My daughter had turned thirty the previous day, and her friend and I had arranged a surprise party at our home for the coming weekend. For once, Mr Smith could be there. He had to go to bed for a couple of hours during the afternoon, but he was with the family to celebrate, and that felt better for us all.

He was weak but the deep dark blue eyes gleamed. It was a particularly warm and early spring, and we were able to spend a lot of time outdoors. I cooked breakfast and brought it to him, sometimes in bed and sometimes on the patio where we could appreciate the garden and enjoy the sun on our faces. In the evenings we wrapped up in blankets, admired the sunsets and, later, gazed at the stars.

It was while we were enjoying the late afternoon sun that the call came to say that Mr Smith Senior's time in this life had reached a peaceful end. It was April 16th, two years to the day since we had heard the word 'tumour' for the first time in relation to Mr Smith.

We couldn't go to the funeral. It was five hundred miles away and we were five days away from our departure date. It would take two days to drive there and two more to drive back, and even if there had been time, Mr Smith just wasn't strong enough.

The family understood. Nothing more could be done for his dad; he had to do what he could for himself now. It was what Mr Smith Senior wanted for him.

I had never held him more closely than I did that night.

Interlude

Monday April 21st 2014
8.10pm
Lima, Peru

We have to run.

The airline promised us a wheelchair and assistance, and both were forthcoming in Amsterdam, but here, where we really need it, we're left to our own limited resources.

We have a wheelchair, but we also have a loaded luggage trolley and I have only one pair of hands. We're late and our connecting flight is due to leave imminently. He has no choice but to get up and walk.

A woman offers directions to the check-in desk. We have to run, she says, there's no time.

I try to tell her he can't run, but I don't think she hears me, so he runs. We follow her out of the building to avoid the crowds. Back inside, she persuades the check-in assistant to let us through, and now we're running again.

My heart aches for this extra stress on his body but there's no time to feel it so we pay the woman for her trouble and dash to the gate. Finally we're where we need to be to take the last step – the last step of the geographical part of our journey – and we're relieved.

Part II

South America

1

Follow the Brown Dirt Road

22nd – 23rd April 2014

The Peru that Mr Smith wanted to visit is a diverse and magical place full of hot springs, dense jungles, beautiful cities and sacred sites. Pucallpa has none of those things. Pucallpa is dusty, dirty and primitive, and it was our new home.

These small absences were of no matter though; we weren't there to admire the views. We could do the tourist trail later, if there was anything left in the budget at the end of it all. For now, we were relieved to have come this far, and we were looking forward to the next chapter with excitement and optimism and trepidation.

Our host Silvia met us at the airport. A well-travelled Italian who had settled in Peru and made it her business to develop an intimate knowledge of the local shamanic scene, she had assured us that the best practitioners of ancient medicines were from this part of the country. There were countless treatment centres in more exotic locations like the Sacred Valley to the south and Iquitos to the north, but, she told us, their best shamans were recruited mainly from Shipibo families from around Pucallpa. The Shipibo-Conibo tribespeople have an unbroken lineage in the ancient art of *curanderismo*, or traditional healing, and their services are highly desired among North American and European spiritual seekers. In response to this modern demand, many of them are now focused on business, and some of them can and do command alarmingly big bucks.

We would have access to the same, or maybe even higher, standards of expertise but without the hefty price tag. We would be focused purely on caring for Mr Smith while the healers did their job of getting him better. And yes, it could be done. It would take as long as it would take but Silvia had seen miracles performed by the very people we'd be meeting in the coming days. She herself had been close to death when she'd arrived four years earlier.

She introduced us to members of the team she had gathered for us: her niece Luisa, who had been hired to cook and clean, and Emilio, a local man who would provide transport in his mototaxi – a motorbike with a rickshaw attached, the most common mode of transport in Pucallpa. We were attracted to the novelty of that, and a bit disappointed to be taken to our hotel by people carrier along with several other weary travellers. We wouldn't miss out though – in the weeks to come there would be plenty of opportunity to enjoy the unique and dubious pleasures of dust in our eyes, grime on our clothes and zero vehicle suspension. Meantime, the warmth in the welcome assured us that we were in the company of like minds and sympathetic hearts.

As we drove along, taking in the otherness of the environment, I wondered whether I could get used to the heat. It was 10pm and it had been dark for five hours, but it was still as hot as my northern blood could endure. Mr Smith had travelled more widely than I had and could adapt, and yes, so could I. I'd come this far with him and I'd do whatever was necessary to see it through.

At the beginning at least, we did feel a bit like tourists. We were spending the night in the hotel because our new home was on a lagoon on the Ucayali River, a tributary of the Amazon, and at this time of year the dirt tracks were under water, with the only access by boat. Our hosts had shown up to meet us wearing boots and bearing a large oar apiece; they were going to find their own way home in the darkness of the night. They would come back in the morning to escort us via one of the local motorboats for hire.

Meantime, Silvia flirted with Mr Smith, and Mr Smith, charmingly to my eye, didn't notice that he was being flirted with. He would be in the care of four beautiful women, she said (there was a second domestic supporter waiting at home), and would want for nothing in the way of feminine comfort and attention. That would provide the basis of care that he needed while the *curanderos* concentrated on his healing.

She had arranged for us to stay in the best room in the hotel, the one that proudly boasted a Jacuzzi and a minibar. It would be a shame to waste them: we were only staying for one night and we had been warned that, although every effort was being made for us, the standards of comfort in the average Peruvian home were different. So, spent as we were from a journey of over twenty-four hours, we sank into the bubbles together and shared a modest bottle of beer. This would be our last taste of luxury for a long time, and we savoured it.

Our first mototaxi ride, to the lagoon, was short, sticky and grimy. In daylight, the town was not pretty, but it did have colour going for it. It reminded me of Mr Smith's remark the previous day. On the flight from Amsterdam to Lima, he'd gestured out of the window to the Andes below, grinned like only he could grin, and said,

'We're not in Scotland anymore, Toto…'

We surely weren't. Just like Toto and Dorothy, we were in a strange land of garish colours that clashed, with each other and sometimes with us. It was a land of brashness and noise. This was the land in which, like Toto and Dorothy, we would encounter strange beings and stranger challenges. We would face our fears head-on and reveal ourselves to be stronger than we knew.

This was the land from which we would find our way home.

First, there was the yellow brick road to follow. Though in our case, it began with more of a brown dirt road and what looked like a browner and dirtier river.

Boarding the boat with its makeshift canopies of discarded

sheets of plastic and its weathered wooden benches, we were beginning to see the reality of what we'd been told to expect. Standards were different here, and though our new home was considered luxurious – it boasted running water, electricity and a flush toilet – it wouldn't be what we were used to. That was okay, we told ourselves, because when your only focus is to get a job done, your surroundings tend to blur into invisibility. Anyway, how bad could it be?

At first sight, worse than expected. In the novel heat, we were just beginning to relax into the journey, trailing our fingers in the cool water and thinking what a shame that those derelict wooden shacks along the shore were spoiling the view, when the boatman steered towards, then moored alongside, the most precarious-looking of them.

It was a wonder, this house, in that it was still standing. High above the lagoon, propped up on stilts that looked suspiciously rotten, its balcony overhung the water. Beneath it, baling out a rowing boat, was a wild woman, a lean, powerful and earthy Amazonian goddess with a smile as big as her heart would turn out to be. This was our first sighting of Claudia, the Columbian *ayahuasquera* who would be our domestic support, nurse and holder of ceremonial space.

As we climbed the steps at the back of the house, they warned us against using the fenced porch that ran the length of the building. It was overdue for repair and the rotting wood could give way under our weight. We weren't tempted to take the risk; the old, stained, bright green porcelain toilet, rust-ridden barbecue and other assorted detritus weren't exactly beckoning us.

The interior was contrastingly agreeable though, and the goddesses' efforts for our comfort were apparent in the room they had prepared for us. For privacy, the window to the kitchen and main living area had been covered with the traditional Shipibo embroidery that was to become familiar. The glassless windows were covered in mosquito mesh and makeshift plastic blinds installed against the worst of the storms that had been troublesome lately. This room was small and basic but it was not uncomfortable really, if we could lay aside our usual expectations – and of course we could, in appreciation that things were different here. Things were different but this was real hospitality and we were glad of it. Our hearts did sink slightly at the sight of the twin beds but we could always push them together, and that small disappointment was overshadowed by our blossoming gratitude.

The house generally reminded me of the scenes in the old Doris Day film *Calamity Jane,* where Jane is joined in her log cabin by the frilly and feminine actress and suddenly the place is transformed with flowers and pretty curtains. This was certainly a run-down wooden structure, but it was a richly decorated run-down wooden structure. In this case, rather than gingham and roses, the adornments were the accoutrements of the *ayahuasquera.* Intricate Shipibo wall-hangings, strings of beads and feathers, sticks of Palo Santo and bottles of *Agua de Florida*; tools of the shaman's trade served the additional purpose of creating a welcoming atmosphere.

Something that alarmed us both at first was that everybody was smoking. We were no longer used to this, and we were dismayed at the incongruity of a place of healing infused with cigarette smoke. We'd heard of *mapacho,* the pure tobacco used by shamans as a sacred medicine, but we didn't know much about it. We were reassured when they told us, and we quickly found out for ourselves that these cigarettes are clean, odour-free and very different to the nicotine varieties that so repelled us. Over the coming weeks, we lifelong non-smokers would even have a few puffs ourselves in the context of ayahuasca ceremonies. Our commitment to healthful recovery was opening our minds and increasing our willingness to engage in whatever practices were in harmony with the treatments we had come here for.

The same principle applied to food: we would act on local advice about what would work best both with Mr Smith's constitution and with the medicines. Our research and our own limited experience had taught us that diet is a crucial component of a shamanic healing process, and in any case we were in no position to insist on our own regime. The new diet was to begin immediately, and in the early afternoon we were introduced to Claudia's culinary skills and Silvia's nutritional standards. It hardly surprised us that these differed from ours, but we *were* surprised by the apparent overuse of sugar, vegetable oils and refined salt. But Silvia's careful attentiveness to our individual needs impressed us and we were willing to unlearn everything we knew about eating for health. We'd been resigned to bland food and restricted intake, so the tasty and abundant lunch was an unexpected pleasure, and we were ready to embrace the whole package; we would put aside some of our own ideas of what was healthy and we'd accede to the experts and to the wisdom of the plants themselves.

In the ceremony room, a recess that led from the dining area and opened out onto the balcony over the river, half a dozen mattresses were laid out and covered with patterned blankets. A plastic mesh hammock hung above them and various pipes and bowls lay half-hidden in corners. I baulked slightly at the animal skin on the floor, and I never did get used to touching it, but the when-in-Rome attitude prevailed regardless. In the coming days we would be introduced to some of the indigenous healers who would be working with us in this space, which would also serve as a living area, reading nook and treatment room.

For now though, exhausted by the newness of everything, including the strange novelty of having no responsibilities for a while, we pushed the single beds together, erected our double mosquito net over and around them, and slept deeply, entwined beneath the gaudy blankets.

2

Settling In

Late April 2014

The absence of responsibilities felt strange and unfamiliar; relaxing isn't easy when you're not used to it. Here we were faced with the unnamed, unanticipated task of finding equilibrium between autonomy and trust, and it began with those single beds.

Back home, during our many preparatory Skype calls with Silvia, we'd been tenacious in our pursuit of answers. Would there be room for self-direction, or would we be expected to place ourselves completely into the hands of the *maestros*?

We'd been reassured. We would be offered the very best of care, treatment and advice that ancient Amazonian lore could offer, and it was all optional. We needn't be concerned about differences of cultural etiquette: nobody would be offended if we declined.

We'd taken care to research the treatment options presented to us back home; we'd asked questions, weighed up alternatives and only then had we allowed our intuition the final say. We'd used all the tools and materials available to us to reach our decisions, and now… well, it wasn't so much that decisions were out of our hands than that everything was taken care of so there were no decisions for us to make.

That didn't just apply to treatment options; every little thing had been taken in hand, including where and how we would sleep. Silvia did say she'd considered giving us a double bed, but she'd been unsure of Mr Smith's level of comfort and whether he would need to sleep alone. He'd done enough of that in Germany, but it wasn't a problem – we could just push the beds together. We were lucky to have beds at all.

We had beds and we had mosquito nets. The air conditioning in the hotel had kept the little monsters away but here, we needed our nets. During the night and for three hours or so at dusk (which seemed unreasonably early at 5pm), we needed to make sure we were under them, Silvia said, in our jeans and socks and long sleeves, and with every millimetre of exposed flesh covered in repellent.

I was conscientious about this, so I assumed that the intense itching that developed on my arms and legs must have been caused by a heat rash. I'm a northern European to the core and I never was good in the heat, especially when I'd taken advice to cover up in dense fabrics.

My assumption was wrong. It took a few days to realise that in the early morning, before we woke, the mosquitos were making their way upwards through the gap between the mattresses and, unfazed by the super-strength lotion, feasting on me. They didn't seem interested in Mr Smith. Perhaps cancerous bodies carry their own natural mosquito repellent. If so, it was one thing to be thankful for, but as for me, large areas of my body were soon covered in big, red, open sores. It didn't just itch, it hurt – more than I could have anticipated – and when Silvia tried to reassure me with the story of Luisa, who'd suffered similarly but who'd become immune after a month or so, I failed to find comfort. A *month*? I couldn't bear this for another minute! Added to the pain was the knowing that my pain was nothing compared to Mr Smith's, the knowing that I was willing to endure whatever came my way in the name of his healing, and the knowing that none of this information stopped me from feeling pathetically sorry for myself.

As it turned out, in my case it would take much longer than a month, and it was a blessing not to know it then. What good would I have been to Mr Smith without hope of relief? And anyway looking back on that time, I barely register the memory of that particular agony. It *was* agony but it was agony of a lesser order.

At the time, belief in an early recovery just about made it bearable. Meantime we tried to improvise a solution with a second mosquito net under the mattresses, but none of our ideas worked, and eventually we had to succumb to the solitude of single beds. The extra net we'd brought turned out to be unusable, so Silvia lent Mr Smith a spare one of hers – this was her winter weight one, less a net and more a construction of dense cotton sheeting. It made of Mr Smith's bed an isolation chamber of sorts. His constant pain made it out of the question for him to squeeze into a single bed with me, so, reluctantly, we relinquished the comfort of holding each other when we finally got the chance to be alone at night.

The nights presented our only chance of being alone. It became obvious early on that this house was less of a private home and more of a gathering-place for friends, friends of friends, passing *gringos* and the Shipibo women who targeted them as buyers for their abundant crafts. People would often show up in the early morning, and as our door opened out onto the kitchen and living area, we were both self-conscious about leaving our room. We were used to conducting our relationship in private, and certainly to going from the bedroom to the shower unobserved. But we'd faced difficulties far greater, and anyway, maybe we'd been too precious about the need for seclusion. We had agreed to a when-in-Rome attitude: this was not, after all, our home and these were not our rules.

For Mr Smith, living by someone else's rules was a relief as much as a challenge, because he was too small an entity to take responsibility for the enormous task of keeping himself alive. He hadn't given in – there were still things to be done, efforts to be made and prayers to be offered. But he had given up, to the higher power that held him. He'd been on the brink of surrender many times but now he was ready to accept whatever outcome was inevitable. It was an attitude of mind that birthed a state of grace in him, and that was awe-inspiring to me – or it would have been if I'd been able to fully share in it. As it was, I was still woefully human and scared.

I still clung to the possibility of recovery – we had so much love to live for – while he relaxed into acceptance. That acceptance allowed him respite that showed in the serenity of his smile and the glow in the deep blue eyes. As I rocked him in his hammock, and we spoke sweet, soft secrets, my fear melted away in the certainty that he was healing.

We both had certainty: his from an almost-familiar kind of knowing that all was well, and mine from my ardent hope that all *would be* well. Our certainty allowed us to trust in those we met over the coming weeks, however exotic and strange their methods looked to our developed-world eyes. We'd trusted in our story so far; it had brought us to this fantastical world of psychedelic Technicolor, and these extraordinary characters would prove worthy of their place in it. Amidst it all, our thread was still glittering, now with added rainbow colours.

It seemed that our only task was to create a bubble of calm amidst a chaotic household whose ethos felt uncomfortably permissive at times. Silvia's insistence that we treat the place like home was kindly meant but harder to implement than we ever acknowledged to ourselves. We were guests, and it was up to us to adapt to the frequent visitors (some of whom operated a hard-sell system and saw us as both curiosities and prospective buyers of their wares), Silvia's volatile temperament and the incessant raucous music booming across the bay from the café bar. But our intimacy was of a different kind now; we found ways to allow it to play out in full view, cherishing a new kind of privacy that didn't require withdrawal from the household.

Silvia was keen to promote the advantages of an all-female household to us both. As well as having all his domestic needs met, Mr Smith's healing would be enhanced, inevitably, by the presence of such beauty, and I would be supported by a sisterhood of spiritually aware and sympathetic attendants while I rested and devoted all my time and energy to his care.

She was missing an important factor. Mr Smith's nurturing side was well developed, and we enjoyed a mutuality that allowed us to be both carer and cared-for. Just being in his presence was enough for me, and moral support, however kindly intended, from people we'd just met was not only unnecessary but it often felt intrusive. Being together and in close quarters with these new people wasn't always entirely comfortable for any of us. Silvia assumed our near-complete ignorance on matters such as nutrition, yoga, bodywork and what was good for us, and often treated us with disdain. After all our learning over the years, that stung, and we both found her hard to warm to at times. As the weeks progressed she would gradually reveal the wounded animal within herself, and we would begin to understand. For now, *our* wounded animals reacted with resentment, but… she'd opened her home to us and she was ready to share her knowledge. That *must* have come from the heart. We decided to focus on that, and we could overlook what were, after all, only minor differences of personality.

Still, there was some unease, and in those first few days we swung often between gratitude and irritation. But we'd come to do a job. There was no energy to be spared on repairing petty disharmony, so we drifted above it, not looking down.

3

Finding Our Place

April – May 2014

It wasn't clear, to begin with, whether Silvia had a particular gift for networking or whether we were living in such a close-knit community that everyone knew everyone else. Either way, her knowledge of the shamans and *curanderos* in the region was encyclopaedic and she appeared on friendly terms with all of them. It was useful to have so many contacts, particularly since her own *maestro*, Tobias, was going to be unavailable for the first few weeks. He was about to leave for Eastern Europe, where his services were in demand. Silvia would have been happiest working with him, but there was no question about the competence of the others. While Tobias was away, we could pick and choose from the rest according to our needs – or Silvia could. No expensive treatment centre could offer us such richness, or such levels of comfort. Fate was looking after us.

Most of the shamans were Shipibo, and almost invariably related to each other: the elder who lived in the suburb just along the riverbank and ran a retreat centre brimming with young foreigners; his wife, also a healer, who worked mainly with the local women; the husband and wife team from the other side of town; the man who'd benefited most from the surge in psychedelic tourism and whose wrists hung with gold watches and bracelets. All of these were to be encountered at various times, often accompanied by assorted children and other relatives whose identities were mysterious to us. They sat round the table on plastic tub chairs procured from the local bars, smoking *mapacho*, drinking coffee and holding court. Less obtrusive but just as interesting was Horacio, the young Ashaninka shaman who'd been lost in the jungle and given up for dead at the age of fourteen. When he'd somehow made his way home two or three weeks later, the villagers had mistaken him for a ghost and run from him in terror. It was an intriguing story, the reality of which, and the subsequent effect on his life, we could only guess at.

A date was set for our first ayahuasca ceremony. It was to be conducted by José, who came recommended by Claudia with excited enthusiasm. With twenty years' experience under her belt, she was a good judge – she'd worked with José a lot and she couldn't think of anyone better. That was enough for us. First, though, there were practical matters to attend to.

We hadn't brought towels, and there weren't any spare for us to use. It seemed that all the towels in the household, as well as the soap and quite a lot of the crockery, bore the insignia of the hotel we'd stayed in on our first night. We were slightly uneasy about that – a minor issue but did it perhaps betray a difference of ethical standards? We put it aside – we weren't here to judge and anyway, we weren't familiar with the norms here. We were learning fast though.

Emilio, who was expected to be at Silvia's beck and call and who always obliged, drove us into town in his mototaxi and dropped us off at the shops to buy towels. In a half-shop, half-market-stall, we managed to find some that weren't too offensively garish. Making our way to the desk to pay for them, we were obstructed by a man balancing on his toes on a chair and welding something to the wall, with no mask and no other form of bodily protection. He smiled broadly at us and gestured for us to pass, while the flames whooshed and sparked inches from his face. We found another route to the desk, exchanging incredulous looks and shaking our heads as if to shake away the thought of what might happen.

What might happen didn't seem to occur to Pucallpan minds, and what seemed to us like an outrageous disregard for safety was evident everywhere. The roads were occupied by mototaxis and motorbikes, often carrying families of four or five, with babies dangling on hips and primly dressed grandmas hugging onto backs. I never saw a helmet, but I did once see a child wearing a paint bucket on his head, so it seemed that people were doing what they could with what they had. Chatting about this later, possession of towels having allowed us, finally, to make full use of the frog-infested shower cabin, we were impressed by this apparently innate fearlessness. We pondered the influence of attitude on outcomes. Mr Smith could relate the welding incident to his own case: though much less rash in his approach, his assumption that all was well – the absence of any thought of disaster – carried a power that he could… well, not use to his advantage exactly; this was hardly a game. But it was good to have his convictions reflected in this small way, and whatever came to pass from now on, he felt safe.

It was that sense of safety that allowed him to relax into trust. Trust in the intuition that had brought us here, to this place, among these people who would support us in our healing. *Our* healing. And because he trusted, I trusted. The horrors of the consulting rooms back in Europe were a million miles away now. All of *that* was irrelevant; it was of another world. It had nothing to do with us now. Now we were here, and here was exactly where we needed to be.

Mr Smith was given his place at the head of the table, on the only chair that wasn't made of bright and brittle plastic. It was interestingly crafted and uncomfortable, and for once he would have preferred the plastic, but this was a place of honour and the flatbreads and cheeses that the women made fresh each morning were ample compensation. Afterwards he would enjoy his smoothie on the balcony where he could put his feet up and admire the view across the river to the treescape beyond. We tried not to notice the general grubbiness in which breakfast was produced, or the occasional scuttling cockroach. The when-in-Rome reflex was strengthening, and what would have been completely unacceptable at home was just the way things were now.

Some things were always going to be unacceptable though, and our association with José lasted only one night. It was our first experience of an authentic ayahuasca ceremony, conducted in complete darkness. I thought that the shaman's hand sweeping across my breasts was accidental, even the second time. Direct engagement with individual participants was part of the process; physical contact was not unexpected and he could easily have missed his target in the dark. Maybe he meant to touch my throat or forehead. I really didn't think anything of it, but later, when I asked Silvia why he had left us so soon, she told me that he'd been sent away after he'd touched both her and Luisa in ways that were not welcome and certainly not part of the work of the traditional healer.

We'd heard about this sort of thing, of course. Even the most casual of investigations into the development of South American shamanism will yield a dozen cautionary tales. The recent interest in the craft among young and affluent North Americans and Europeans, and the sudden perceived abundance of money and sex, have encouraged an industry that is perhaps not always the most honourable, and no doubt there are many 'shamans' with dubious claims on the title. This was not the case with José, who had never given any cause for concern in all the years Claudia had known and admired him. Silvia supposed that, like too many others, he'd allowed his baser instincts to get the better of him in response to the influx of *gringos* with cash in their pockets and a hunger for the exotic. He wouldn't last much longer in respectable circles, she said, and it was a shame. But his behaviour would not be tolerated, and she was now considering who should be invited to work with us in the future.

She didn't have to consider for long, as it turned out, because a few days later we learned that Tobias, who would always have been her first choice, had had a change of plan and would be available for the next few weeks after all. Within minutes, he and his wife Manola were drinking coffee and smoking *mapacho* at the kitchen table, and discussing the best course of action for Mr Smith. Silvia was the image of relieved satisfaction; Fate had it all in hand once again.

It was at this meeting that the potential for clashes with Silvia became uncomfortably clear. Translating Tobias' terms and conditions for us, she stressed what a great deal we were being offered – he was asking for much less than we might reasonably expect to pay – and we should grab the opportunity. We were appreciative but hesitant. We'd been clear at the outset – we had a limited pot of money; there was only my very modest pension coming in now and we were still paying rent on a four-bedroom house back home, so careful budgeting was essential. She didn't seem to understand that appreciating a bargain was not the same as being in a position to accept it. Besides, we hadn't said no – we just needed to think things through.

She got angry. She had before, and she would again. It was clear by now that Silvia's anger was never very far from the surface, and we often walked on eggshells. We managed, finally, to get through to her that our hesitancy wasn't a bargaining technique to get Tobias to lower his price; that our caution was necessary and shouldn't be understood as ingratitude. Mr Smith kept his cool – but I felt he shouldn't have had to. Tobias understood, though, and of course – because Fate was in charge now – we were able to come to an arrangement that compromised neither party.

Under Tobias' guidance, I was to administer some plant medicines that he would prepare for Mr Smith. There was medicine for me, too, to build my strength and deal with the remnants of my old illness. Tobias and Manola would conduct an ayahuasca ceremony every few days, and there was even a lotion made of camphor and alcohol for my mosquito bites.

Within the same tribes and even within the same families, there are differences of flavour in ceremonial work. Mr Smith wasn't drinking ayahuasca for the first few ceremonies – he wasn't ready for that yet – but he did take part and we both grew to love Tobias' particularly gentle singing style. Icaros are shamanic songs said to have been taught to early *ayahuasqueros* by the plant spirits themselves, and they are sung in ceremony to support and strengthen the effects of the medicine. There is an irresistible power in the practice, and Tobias' icaros were the best of them all. Tobias was also one of the few remaining *maestros* skilled at sucking out pain from the body. We were sceptical of this but it did seem to work. Anything that soothed and comforted Mr Smith was a good thing in my estimation, and the absence of pain he reported during ceremony was blissful for us both.

It puzzles me that there's a flourishing tourist industry in ayahuasca, because it's neither easy nor pleasurable. It tastes disgusting and it becomes more disgusting as time goes on. It can trigger a strong gag reflex and cause unspeakable nausea which culminates in violent vomiting if you're lucky – and that's not to mention the terrifying visions and the sense of loss of self. Add to all of this the horror of fast-moving cockroaches, mantises and spiders in the dark, and you'll begin to understand why I was never sure that I wanted to take it. There was something compelling about it though, and something cleansing – the contents of my bucket at the end of the night were definitely not worth holding on to. At the end of each ceremony we felt a profound sense of peace; some of my favourite memories are of lying perfectly still while being serenaded by Tobias' ethereal voice and watching the dance of the fireflies through the mesh on the ceiling. When it was all over and I could trust my legs to carry me, I picked my way over to Mr Smith's mat, where I wrapped him in his blanket and held him, gently hugging his back and no longer caring that I was leaning against the wall most likely to be infested with bugs. Later, we would break our fast with tiny sweet bananas, holding hands on the balcony, enjoying the silence and absorbing the view of the moonlight playing on the water and the trees beyond. Here we would share our experiences quietly before going to our separate beds, stopping to say goodnight to Kevin, the tiny lizard who had taken up residence on our wall. We'd named him Kevin for the fun of it – it was hard not to keep a sense of fun in the presence of Mr Smith, and we were agreed that he did look like a Kevin. These were rare moments; cherished gifts from the spirit of ayahuasca, who showed us a new glittering thread, reflected in the colourful darting lights that lingered at the fringes of our shamanic nights and welcomed us both to slumber.

4

Finding Our Way

May 2014

Silvia took control. She had the contacts and the local knowledge, and she knew how much things cost so she took note of our budget and worked out a plan. There was nothing to worry about, she told us: we had more than enough to pay our share of the domestic expenses, cover the cost of Mr Smith's treatment and probably even have some money left over to see the sights of this country we'd settled in.

We wondered whether she really was in control. There was no way of knowing how long it would all take, so no way of knowing how long our money would have to last. How can anyone budget on that basis? It was pointless to challenge her though, in the face of her indignant and wounded protestations at anything that she might interpret as criticism. Besides, courteous and appreciative guests don't aggravate their hosts, and we weren't inclined to rock the boat.

She insisted that, once we were ready to go home, we would do so only to pack up our house, sell all our possessions and return to Peru to continue Mr Smith's treatment. She impressed on us, again and again, how important this was to his recovery. We could make a permanent home here, where we would be in demand as English teachers and would have a high standard of living. We didn't want to be English teachers and we'd finally reached a stage in life where we were never again going to be anything we didn't want to be. We were too fond of our family and our pets to move away to the other side of the world, and the prospect of life without winters and springs almost distressed us. We were already longing for cool summers and long, light evenings. None of these considerations deterred Silvia though;

she was adamant and imperious.

Meantime, having taken control, she made a decision on our behalf that introduced an impossible dilemma. I was to go home, alone, on May 21st. We had return tickets and she wanted to salvage something; she felt bad that we had wasted our money. I was to go home, downgrade to the most modest home I could find, get a job – any job – and live as frugally as I could possibly manage, on potatoes and lentils if need be, so that I could send money over for Mr Smith. Her anger was roused again when we expressed a preference to stay together. We could see the reasoning behind the plan, but it fell short of workable in our view. There was no point in protesting though – that much, we'd learned.

Silvia was in charge and I was to go home. The last thing we wanted or needed was to be apart at this moment – nothing was clearer than that. Separation was unthinkable, and going back to Europe together, back into the hands of allopaths who didn't believe in Mr Smith's recovery, was just as unthinkable. All along I had entertained a notion of us returning to Scotland together, healthy and robust, making our way through airports hand-in-hand; my head resting on his shoulder during flights; the welcoming delight on the faces of loved ones to greet us at the end of the journey. The thought of any other outcome was unbearable. Bearing the unbearable had almost become second nature by now, but this was differently unbearable – unbearably so. What could we do though? We were there at Silvia's invitation and it seemed that her invitation to me was due to expire. I was being asked to leave, and he couldn't leave with me, because until he was healed, there was nowhere for him to go. I wasn't to worry though, according to Silvia – I was leaving him in capable hands and she would care for him and send him home to me wholly healed and happy.

I didn't believe her because by now I didn't believe she was in control. She had no control over the turmoil that she had unthinkingly unleashed, and she had no real power to heal him. How could he heal in the hands of this angry woman? She could massage his feet and rock his hammock and sing icaros to him, but there was no healing magic in any of it. Our faith in her was wavering but our faith in his healing never did. He had let go of the reins, and no human hand could steer them in the direction he was to take – not ours, not Silvia's, not any or all of the *maestros'*. It was comforting to remember that, and to give up any thought of how it was going to work out. Our intuition was stronger than Silvia's notions of how things had to be. It would all be okay.

And it was. The unseen hands guided the reins smoothly, and by the time May 21st came and went, they'd swept a mist of amnesia around the plan to send me home. By now we were established in a routine of medicines (some surprisingly tasty and some definitely not), nightly poultices administered expertly by Claudia, and vomitivas. This is the practice of drinking a sugar cane concoction followed by several litres of warm water, at speed, then vomiting copiously, all to Silvia's braying encouragement. At first, Tobias prescribed this for me, to purify the blood and address the bites that now dappled almost every body part, and soon enough Mr Smith was joining me. Nothing says togetherness quite like leaning over a balcony to expel stomach contents in harrowing tandem, and by now it was impossible to separate us.

Not even the sleeping arrangements could separate us. Awakened at 6am by the PA system blaring from across the bay (a sort of compulsory local radio station with a very limited playlist and a very ebullient presenter), our view of each other was blocked by the dense cotton of the mosquito nets. An unspoken agreement came into play, that a hand pressed against the fabric signalled 'I'm awake and I'm ready to connect with you'. One palm would be met by another in a new ritual that spoke of much more than our sleepy minds could find words for. It was our best substitute for warm, soft morning cuddles and to compensate for that lack, we poured every gift our hearts held through our bodies and pressed them through those outstretched palms.

After breakfast there was a prescribed daily walk along the riverbank now that the waterline had gone down and the path was clear. We could hold hands again and talk nonsense, just like we had on our daily dog walks at home. We could talk nonsense and perfect sense; we could make idle plans for the future; we could share opinions and diffuse the petty stresses of communal living; we could admire the butterflies. We could walk less now, and much more slowly – Mr Smith's strength was ebbing. Sometimes, when he needed a break, we would sit on a fallen branch and watch the local men building boats. Sometimes we would stop and watch the micro-world of ants and spiders hurrying busily while we rested. Often we sat in the shade of the canopy next to the house, making friends with the dogs and chickens and turkeys, delaying the climb up the battered timber staircase.

Returning from one such outing, we were greeted by Tobias, who had come to let us know that his plans had changed again. A large group of Europeans was coming to stay at the jungle centre he ran together with Manola's family. They'd be there for two weeks and as a senior member of the shamanic team, he was needed. He had our case in hand though: he had brought a friend with him. This was Alejandro and he was here to meet us and to talk things through with Tobias and Silvia. Alejandro would be taking Tobias' place for a while. He was well qualified and well briefed; his was a safe pair of hands.

The morning walks are fused together in my memory now, except for the one that broke with routine; that one stands out because of the way it began and because of the content of the discussion and the strength of the emotion that carried it.

Silvia was quick to criticise, and the attitudes of the locals were often in the firing line. They were inclined, if not to lie, to overstate their promises, and they weren't above theft if they saw that you had more than they had. Most people here lived in poverty and they were happy to take from you to even things up a little if they could. That, in a nutshell, was the Peruvian way according to Silvia. True to the principle that we attract what we expect, and with Silvia monitoring our lifestyle and our movements so closely, this was being borne out in our experience at times. I'd resorted to doing our own washing (by hand, in a tub of cool water) after the second instance of clothes disappearing from the pile sent back from the laundry; and I'd been told, 'No, we don't have that in another colour,' in a shop, only to find the item in *two* other colours a few moments later.

On one of our occasional shopping trips Silvia had taken me to a place that sold cropped tops to replace the lingerie that had vanished from the laundry pile. I'd come back with three such tops in three different sizes, despite the assistant's emphatic assurance that they were all the same. I discovered this next morning and agreed with Silvia, quite mildly I thought, that some Peruvian shop assistants will bend the truth to secure a sale.

Her response was explosive. We'd seen it before, a week or two earlier, when she'd banished Luisa over what looked like a minor disagreement. Luisa had retaliated and, next day, she'd left quietly. Silvia had dismissed the incident as hot air, the volatile Italian temperament. It was the other side of a valuable coin: the nurturing warmth in the hearts of these women was tangible, so we tried to accept their volatility as a quirky counterbalance – but it did unsettle us.

It unsettled us more when I was the one on the receiving end. By now the valve on my own inner pressure cooker was ready to blow and I struggled to stay calm. She said I was ungrateful and insulting; I said I'd said no more than she'd said herself. She said

I was overspending on the budget anyway; I said I hadn't bought anything she hadn't encouraged me to buy, and that she was treating us like children: how dare she keep track of every penny we spent of our own money? Voices got louder. Shouting took place. Screaming may have taken place. Mr Smith emerged from the bedroom and took me in his arms. At the sight of him, I dissolved. He needed a calm environment; he had always been sensitive to violent emotion and this was not helping him get better. It wasn't helping any of us and I couldn't stay under this roof another moment. I fled, hoping to calm myself with a solitary walk.

Of course, I didn't get very far before I thought of Mr Smith, left behind. I knew he was even more sensitive to aggression than I was, so I went back to get him. I found him in the doorway of Silvia's bedroom (she had invited him in – the flirting was ongoing), trying to calm her. He agreed that a walk would be a good idea, and we ambled along the riverbank together.

Claudia had witnessed it all, he told me, and as far as he could make out with his limited understanding of Spanish, she had chastised Silvia, and Silvia had protested, then conceded. I was still shaken. I didn't want to go back. I wanted to leave, and he did too – it wasn't working out between us and Silvia. The attack had been personal and shocking – I'd been accused of all manner of wrongdoing that I had never intended. I needed Mr Smith's assurance that it wasn't true, and thankfully, I got it. We gave voice to what had been a tentative shared feeling that she resented my presence; it seemed that there were more than practical concerns behind her earlier plan to send me back. We talked of leaving again, this time together. It would be good to go home, but to go home to what? Our family and friends, yes – and oh, we missed them – but the hospitals, the early grave? The invitation to spend a few weeks in Portugal to finish the Kambo treatment was still open, but would there be enough cash in the pot for that? And *that* would take us right to the wire of our last hope. We couldn't afford to get that close. That old fear came flooding back, its edges no less sharp for the familiarity of it. We sat on the fallen branch for a long time that morning.

We were agreed. This was the path we were on and we'd walk right to the end of it. And Silvia wasn't so bad, it was just that we were all under such stress and the fuses were bound to burn down sooner or later. We'd go back to the house and make peace with her. We were decided, but I was apprehensive.

By the time we got back, her mood had changed: we had a guest bearing good news. Alejandro was preparing to move in with us in a few days' time. He was going to stay with Mr Smith round the clock for two weeks, monitoring him closely and giving him twenty-four hour care as needed. During these two weeks he would hold a ceremony on ten consecutive nights. He would ease the pain and work to remove the 'demons' in Mr Smith's body. This was an opportunity beyond anything we could have asked for, and the cost was well under what we would normally be expected to pay. Silvia apologised, and we hugged and agreed to be friends.

5

Going Deeper

May – June 2014

The prospect of ten consecutive nights of drinking ayahuasca was a daunting one, and I was duly daunted. Every day I questioned my motives and every evening I came close to changing my mind. At the outset, I hadn't even been sure that I'd be taking the medicine – we were here for Mr Smith, not for me; this was his path and I was just here to walk it with him. The decision to engage with such a powerful force is an individual one, and more of a calling than a choice. Mr Smith had had the calling; my commitment – my reason for being there – was for him, to be with him while he healed. Still, there was no question among the *maestros* and *ayahuasqueras* about my participation: they, like us, were of the mind that his healing was my healing. And anyway, it came to pass that every evening, the spirit of the medicine *did* call me in.

She called me into my shadows, she showed me parts of myself I'd never wanted to see and she wrenched my guts as she thrust my deepest fears into my face. I asked her to be gentle; she was anything but. I guess I needed to find all of the strength within me to be what Mr Smith needed from me, and I needed it *now*; this was no time to be gentle. I've often heard it said that Mamma Aya always gives us what we need and not what we think we want, and she didn't let me down.

Meantime, the retching noises that emanated from Mr Smith's corner once or twice a night were as reassuring as they were heart-rending. Likewise, his soft encouragement from a few feet away sustained me through many a harrowing pukefest. It was good. It was all good, even when it was awful.

With Tobias and Manola we'd had two or three ceremonies a

week, so we felt like initiates. I had finally dropped my fear of vomiting and by now I even appreciated the benefits of two or even three fingers down the throat. Hideous as the experience was (ayahuasca tastes indescribably foul going down and even more so coming back up), it was preferable to the nausea when the stuff clearly needed to shift but was stubbornly holding on. Mr Smith, well into his stride now, was gaining a reputation in the shamanic community for his fortitude. I had always been proud of this man, but never more so than now. His body was weak but he never was.

The core aspects of the ceremonies were the same as before: the space was cleansed by the burning of Palo Santo (literally 'holy wood') sticks; the lights were extinguished and we drank in turn, then were each given one-on-one time when the *maestro* sat with us to sing. The ubiquitous *Agua de Florida*, an alcohol-based perfume used to cleanse and calm, was still very much in evidence and we had our personal supplies to hand for those moments when it all felt too much. Still, Alejandro was a bit different to what we'd been used to. His methods included rough manipulation of the head and shoulders, and the administering of *mapacho* cigarettes. These were familiar now – the other participants (Silvia, Luisa, Claudia and occasionally Emilio) smoked them in this and almost every other context, and Tobias, in common with other *curanderos*, used it in ritual to purify energies, enable healing and provide a masculine force to balance the feminine spirit of ayahuasca. As non-smokers, we hadn't been offered them before, but now Silvia encouraged us to give them a try. Assured of their purity, we held to the tradition of holding the smoke in the mouth for a few seconds, without inhaling, before slowly releasing it.

Tobias' singing and Manola's infectious giggle were absent now, and we missed them. We were less keen on Alejandro's rasping intonations, and we were all somewhat bemused by his apparent lack of reverence. Silvia had to have a quiet word with him after he took a phone call while administering the medicine one night – it seems that personal phones are relatively new among tribespeople, and that some of them are still learning the etiquette.

By the tenth night my body was protesting so much that the gag reflex kicked in even before my turn came to kneel in front of Alejandro and drink. Discussing this with Silvia, she agreed that I may have gone one ceremony too far, and she reminded me that I could always choose not to partake. I thanked her; I knew that, but by now it was almost harder not to. I wasn't sorry that the ten nights were over though, and I slept a lot the next day. Mr Smith was doing better: the abdominal lumps revealed by his recent weight loss were getting smaller. He was healing, and I would be willing to gag and retch every night for the rest of my life in gratitude for such a gift.

Aside from the ceremonies, we barely saw Alejandro during those ten days. He would emerge for breakfast and lunch but most of the time he stayed in his room or was entirely absent for long hours, gathering the plants to make Mr Smith's daily elixirs. His craft involved so much more than was visible to us; many walking miles were covered unseen, and decades – maybe even centuries – of acquired wisdom were invested in finding exactly the right plants and making the most beneficial choices. Our nightly *muchas gracias Maestros* were sincere in this knowledge, regardless of our preference for Tobias and Manola.

Silvia had an almost childlike gift for enthusiasm, and around day five she announced with excitement that from now on we'd have the benefit of two shamans in our ceremonies. Horacio had been a regular visitor to the house throughout our time there, and Silvia loved him for his willingness to disclose secrets that the Shipibo kept to themselves. Enigmas were exposed, mysteries solved and enchantments revealed. Looking back, the warning sign flashing above Horacio's head was obscured by the dazzle of Silvia's fervour, and we were unalarmed.

Two shamans from different traditions were sold as a double win, and our response was a more-the-merrier one. They would complement each other, and the effect would be magnified. We were all for that, of course, and we were intrigued by the Ashininka ways and how they might differ from what we'd experienced so far.

It might have gone that way, or maybe it was never going to. Maybe – and this does seem more likely in the light of what we were to learn – the subtleties of each approach were always going to be drowned by the noise of the other. As it turned out, there was no subtlety to be discerned above the cacophonous clash of icaros. One night, in the deafening silence when it was all over, Mr Smith likened the noise to *Duelling Banjos*, but louder and less tuneful. Often, Horacio and Alejandro would sing different songs at the same time, seeming to vie for supremacy in a three-way match against the booming beats from the nightclub along the shoreline. It did not feel conducive to healing.

Sometimes I wanted to scream in their faces to shut up. The peace we had come to know in the gentle wake of Tobias' icaros was no longer ours, though thankfully we had the compensatory sweetness of Claudia's voice as she surrendered to her nature. Sometimes, in the few minutes when the shamans were resting, she would ease into song while drifting on her mat beside me, and sometimes we would gradually realise that the haunting melody that seemed to arise from the ether was a gift from the version of Claudia who was now dangling her toes in the river below where we lay. We never heard her leave or return.

She was skilled in massage too, in common with all the women, and she seemed to know exactly when we needed to be soothed beneath her hands. The ceremonies were wordless for the most part, and language was transcended effortlessly; in the hands of Mamma Aya we were all one. At times on those nights the *maestros* felt very 'other' to me, but of course, we were at one with them too; it was just that it wasn't always comfortable to be in our own presence. Mr Smith, though, became more at home within his pained and diminishing body with every evening that passed in this way and with every night of gazing across the water to the black horizon.

Claudia's abilities were not limited to nurturing and singing. She made beautiful jewellery and could turn her hand to just about any practical task. She was impressive with a machete, among other things. We watched her, somewhat awestruck, as she hacked down branches from the trees that arced over the roof, and steeped the leaves in water for us to bathe in. By 'bathe', I mean stand in a large bucket in the shower hut and throw water over each other, rubbing the fractured leaves onto each other's skin. My memories of those rare intimate moments are as vivid and precious as those of our first shower together all those years earlier, and just as affirming. We laughed – me at Mr Smith's easy humour in the face of the ridiculous, and him in delight at making me laugh.

It's hard to remember what plants were used in our herbal baths. The whats and hows and whys of these and the various oral medicines were all explained, and it all made a sort of sense. Silvia was taking notes on everything that was prescribed, and would make sure we had a list to take home. In the end, she couldn't keep the promise and most of the information is missing now. One thing does stand out among the others though – ayahuma, a fruit the size of a large watermelon with a husk as hard as a mature coconut. We watched Horacio cleave them open and we reeled bit at the odour of the black rotting flesh inside. This plant was a perfect partner to ayahuasca, we were told, and its healing properties were potent and varied. It was too strong to ingest but it was good to bathe in. There's a photo of Mr Smith, sitting in the sunshine drying off after his bath. He's smiling broadly and his hair and beard, which are white by now and have begun to grow wild, are blackened where he rubbed this malodorous gloop into them. Mr Smith always was an in-for-a-penny sort of guy; if he was going to do something, he was going to do it thoroughly, and with a certain style.

The days were short and restful; still, no moment went to waste, and relaxed conversations proved educational. As Mr Smith reposed in the hammock in the ceremony room, I attended to our laundry, with particular care for the bandages that Claudia and I wrapped around the herbal poultice each night, and we both chatted amiably with Silvia. She told us of her life and about how she had come to live here and do this. She shared her dreams of a future in which she would create a more tranquil healing centre further from the town, and the three of us discussed ways to fund it. She warned us about *brujers,* those involved in the shamanic arts who choose to work with dark forces, and thanked the Heavens that she knew who they were and how to protect us all from mischievous intent. Later when we were alone, we agreed that Silvia was not all that bad really. 'Not all that bad' was articulated with some affection; being Mrs Smith had taught me that in Smithspeak, quiet understatements carry more than their surface meanings, and I understood what he meant.

Alejandro left promptly at the end of the ten nights, and Horacio faded back into the background. A few days later we returned from our morning walk to find Tobias and Manola with Silvia on the balcony, looking healthy and refreshed, deep in discussion about how it had all gone.

When we spend all our days and nights with someone, we don't notice them change, and when we long for a particular kind of change, we can persuade ourselves that just such a change is coming. Mr Smith was calm, at times serene, and I was hopeful. Tobias had no delusions though; at first sight of Mr Smith he saw a truth that I'd been blind to. He'd been listening to Silvia's account and from what he'd heard, Alejandro hadn't done enough for us. He was already visibly dismayed, and seeing Mr Smith confirmed the impression he'd just formed. More discussion took place, and eventually we were invited to join them on the balcony to hear Tobias' new plan.

Mr Smith was now in need of intensive treatment, with twenty-four hour care and constant monitoring. The only option now was the jungle centre, where three *curanderos* would work in partnership to heal him. Manola's family had extensive and historic experience in curing illness, and they had established this camp some years before. Mr Smith would be attended by Tobias, Manola's father Eduardo, and her brother Ambrosio, Eduardo' eldest son and the heir to his wisdom. They had access to plants that grew in the jungle, and that were needed fresh and in quantities that couldn't easily be transported. Life in the jungle was tough but Mr Smith was resilient and could cope. We were being offered a special financial deal too, but even so, it meant more spending. I was nervous about that but much more nervous about the risks of not taking up this offer – and in any case, there was no other offer. Tobias was the expert, and he felt that this was the only course of action we could take.

Tobias and Eduardo's earlier plans to travel to Russia hadn't been cancelled, only postponed, and they were leaving in mid-June. That gave them a couple of weeks to work with Mr Smith, at which point he would return to Silvia's house and we would all rest for the month they'd be away. Then he would go back to the jungle and complete the healing there. It would astound us, Silvia said, how much difference these healers could make in two weeks. It was all going to work out beautifully.

6

Separation and Succour

June 2014

I'm not sure now who insisted that I stay behind. By now I could follow fairly complex conversations in Spanish, and I think I caught most of what was said out there on the balcony, but I didn't discern any such instruction from Tobias. Silvia was emphatic though: I was *not* to go to the jungle. I wasn't strong enough, and I think she meant strength of character. I was too scared of insects and I wouldn't be able to take the heat. If I thought mosquitoes were a problem here, I would never be able to cope with them in the depths of the jungle. Besides all this, there wasn't enough in the budget for me to go. I could have protested it all, apart from the part about money, and that part was decisive. Besides, I wasn't invited. Silvia would go with him, and she promised to take care of him as well as I could. She really seemed to believe that.

As I remember, we wept that night. Mr Smith was offended on my behalf. He knew me better than anyone and he didn't agree with Silvia's appraisal, which pained him almost as much as the prospect of separation. Fortitude had almost defined the two of us in these last few years, softened by his sensitivity, and to see me judged as lacking strength was hard for him. Fortitude won out though, as is its nature, and we began to galvanize ourselves in preparation. Silvia decided that she and Mr Smith would not eat with the family during those two weeks; she didn't trust them to provide nutritional balance. They were clueless, she said – they had no idea about diet and their food would impede his healing. Praising them to the skies for their ability to heal, then condemning them for their inability to support that healing, seemed to us to be both disrespectful and contradictory.

Still, by now we were used to this sort of talk, and Mr Smith's particular brand of quiet wisdom dictated that we hold our silence. An unwinnable argument just wasn't worth the energy.

I went shopping again. There was an interminable list of things to buy for Mr Smith's comfort: a hammock; enormous laundry bags for the extra bedding; sealable boxes to protect his personal food store from infestation. We were assured that though there was no refrigeration at the centre, there was a 'minimal' standard of hygiene. By now we were unalarmed by minimal standards, though we did wonder how much lower they could be than those we'd lived by so far. Added to this were the tarantulas and deadly snakes lurking in the grass, and the oppressive heat. Still, I wished I was going with them, and so did Mr Smith.

It was a Thursday when they took him away. He hadn't left the house, other than for his short daily walks, since the day we'd shopped for towels six weeks earlier, and the jolting of the mototaxi across the rough terrain along the riverbank was hard on him. Still, the handsome jawline was firm and resolute. Still, here was my Mr Smith, in his strength and glory.

We waited at the port while Silvia fussed and ran last-minute errands and the boat was made ready for the five-hour journey. It had lost its motor only a few weeks earlier, we'd been told, to the pirates who populated these lawless waters. Carrying guns on board was a necessary precaution.

The port was buzzing: Pucallpa is a main distribution centre for commerce and the gateway to Iquitos for travellers and tourists, and the bright awnings of market stalls and the giant topiary sculptures lining the promenade gave it a carnival feel. We ambled slowly along – not too far – and found a shaded spot to sit in and watch the world go by. These were our last few minutes together, in full public view, and for a while I was torn between savouring them and longing for the parting to be over. We had been apart before, of course, but there had always been the phone, and this felt different.

We had expected a passenger boat, with canopies to shade him and benches with backrests to support him, and as we were guided to the bank, we were met by the sight of just such a boat. We should have known better than to have any expectations; as this boat bobbed slowly away from its moorings, it moved just enough to reveal a small rowing boat behind it, customised with a tiny motor at the back, and with Tobias and Manola perched on its edge. Here was the vessel that was to take Mr Smith on his epic voyage.

We stood, hearts lurching, on the bank while Tobias and Emilio loaded the many bags of supplies into the boat to the tune of Silvia's autocratic instruction. When Tobias reached out to steer Mr Smith on board, I stopped him.

'Hey! Where's my hug?'

'Oh, I'd forgotten you weren't coming!'

The embrace was brief – Tobias was tugging on his arm – but we made the best of it and it held all the love in the world between us in those few moments.

There would be no phone calls; there was no reception in the jungle and the nearest village was a bumpy twenty-minute mototaxi journey away. Mr Smith was not going to be able to make that journey until he was significantly better, which he would be by the end of those two weeks. Silvia would make the trip every two days to keep me informed of his progress, and that would have to be enough.

The house became very quiet. Luisa had been welcomed back, tentatively, as a visitor, but had returned to Italy a week or two earlier, and Claudia departed on the same day Mr Smith did. Silvia had arranged for Emilio and his young partner to stay with me to keep me safe and provide transport when needed, but they were out most of the time and kept very much to their room when they were around, so I spent my days alone. I cleaned the kitchen first of all – it was one thing to trust that it was clean while suspecting otherwise, and another thing altogether to believe it in the face of clear evidence to the contrary. By now my Spanish was just about equal to the task of simple food shopping, and on the domestic front life ticked along. I missed Mr Smith from the moment of our final wave, me on the bank and him looking so far away and vulnerable, but it was only going to be for a couple of weeks. We'd survived more than this.

With no Mr Smith to care for, there wasn't much to do, and I'd run out of books. My smartphone app of classic novels kept me occupied, at those times when I could concentrate, and so did the modem that Emilio had brought me so I wouldn't have to go to the hotel in town to get online. Team Smith really came into their own now, via social media and video chat; their outpourings of love and support reached across six thousand miles and into parts of my heart that none of the kind-hearted and generous-spirited souls in this place had been able to find.

Nothing develops intuition more than the absence of communications systems, and though I was nervous, I felt Mr Smith's strength and knew that there was enough of it to see us both through. When the call came two days later, I heard that in ceremony with Eduardo, he'd received some powerful visual messages from ayahuasca. A good shaman works gradually with the medicines: first divine protection is called in, energies are cleansed and healing takes place. Only when the essential first steps are complete does the spirit offer us direct teachings in the form of visual experiences. Now we had a very encouraging sign: although he'd had his share of visions, this one had been much clearer, stronger and more meaningful. I rejoiced, but I longed to hear the story first hand.

My personal journey continued in Mr Smith's absence. Silvia had arranged for Horacio to hold a ceremony for me on alternate nights. A personal shaman for two weeks is unheard of, and undoubtedly beyond what money could buy, but I didn't want it. Horacio's fees were certainly more than reasonable, but this was money we didn't need to spend – I was not the priority here. In any case, I really wanted a break from ayahuasca now. The cleansing action had been harrowing and I'd had enough.

Silvia had insisted that I would experience a breakthrough soon, just as Mr Smith had, and that paying Horacio was within budget. In her absence, I could have cancelled the arrangement, and I almost did – every time Horacio left in the morning, words to the effect of 'please don't come back tomorrow' clung like limpets to the tip of my tongue and remained unsaid.

In Smithspeak, Horacio wasn't so bad really. My biggest gripe was that, when he came to my mat to sing my personal icaro, he insisted that I sat up to face him. This appeared to be Ashaninka etiquette, no matter how wrung out and wobbly I felt, or how firmly my belly was glued to the floor. It took all my resolve to rise and meet him. He repaid my courtesy with kindness though, and often, when the vomiting became really severe, he would come and sing again, and blow smoke over my head and down my body. I was glad of it, though I did miss the women and their soothing hands at times like these. Gradually, I learned to flow from the distress of relentless nausea to the joy of singing his simple icaros, soothing myself under his guidance. I carried on singing softly, on the balcony, into the night. Mamma Aya had songs to teach me, and they helped.

7

Decision Impossible

June 2014

The regular progress reports didn't materialise as promised, and my fear, ever-present beneath the surface, was stark in the lambent daylight. There was no call two days after the first one, or the day after that. I remember pacing the floor a lot, trying to burn off nervous energy. Between times, I sat with my cherished modem and presented an optimistic picture to Team Smith back home. I didn't have to fake it – I believed it. I had to.

I believed it in the face of my fear. I was not yet ready to 'let go and let God' as Mr Smith had done, and so I had no choice but to live by my conscious mind and its conviction that all would be well on its terms. There were no other terms by which all could be well. I can see now that there was much still to be learned, but meantime, I waited for the phone to ring and tried to settle to a new level of normality.

As I remember, there was only one call between the first and last. Mr Smith was doing well. Everyone was impressed by his determination and strength, and his body was responding to the treatments. Did I have a message for him?

'Just tell him I love him…'

It was hardly news to him, but there was nothing more to be said, and the message was urgent. She was to promise to stress it, because it was important for him to hear it again.

More days passed by, after that call. Two, three, four… The calls were to come to Emilio's phone, and as he was so often absent, it would have been easy to miss them. Emilio's local knowledge and grasp of English kept him busy as a driver, guide and promoter of services, to other *gringos* as well as to us. He was perpetually on call and his comings and goings were unpredictable; I had no way of knowing when he would return to the house, and so my preference for solitude vied with my impatience for news. There was the anticipated disappointment that I might have missed a call, and the added apprehension that no news was bad news – that Silvia might have a reason to want to avoid talking to me. It all combined in a strange brew to mix with the ayahuasca and contribute to the relentless churning in my stomach.

Meantime, the mayhem that was life by the lagoon continued. The community's water pipes had burst and were being repaired right behind the house, and one of the neighbours was using a chainsaw and a hammer to build a new boat just under our window. By now I barely noticed the noise, till finally the call came and I had to stand in the shower hut, right at the end of the building, to stand a chance of hearing Silvia's voice.

He particularly wanted her to tell me how thin he'd become. He was even thinner than when he'd had the post-op infection in hospital. He wanted me to know that in advance, to spare me the shock when eventually we'd be reunited.

That wasn't the shocking thing though. That, I could deal with. What Silvia had to say next was what stopped the world in its tracks. She said it in such an ordinary tone that I couldn't quite grasp it at first.

'His condition is critical now.'

I couldn't take it at face value. Maybe because he'd been doing so well. Maybe because she sounded so matter-of-fact and unconcerned, and maybe because her concept of truth was known to be somewhat creative. There was the added factor that she was speaking in a foreign language, and, with an inexplicably rational approach, I addressed this first. Was she sure of what the term meant in English? Yes, she was. Yes, she meant to say exactly that.

Could I believe her? I didn't know. We'd heard her misrepresent people and situations before, for dramatic effect, but this was not the time for even small embellishments. Surely she knew that?

As my frantic mind laboured to make some sense of what she'd said, Silvia was still talking. She understood my impulse to be with him, but Tobias' instructions were clear: I was not to go to the jungle. Mr Smith was so weak that the emotional impact of seeing me could kill him.

Seeing me could kill him. He was a six-hour journey away so even if I set off right now, he could be dead by the time I reached him. That's what 'critical' meant. It meant he could recover, or he could die. And if he didn't die before I could reach him, he might die from the exertion of a reunion.

There was no meaningful decision to be made. I could defy Tobias and go to Mr Smith anyway. I couldn't let him die alone, and without me by his side he would be alone. But if I went to him, that might cause him to die. If I didn't go – if I didn't risk tipping the delicate balance between life and death with my presence – he might get better. My intuition, or my hope, said he was going to get better either way, and that was all I had to go on.

Of course I would go to him; he needed me and I needed him. But to get there and stay there I would need the co-operation of several people, and those we'd relied on to date were unlikely to help me if the *maestro* forbade it. I didn't know how to book a mototaxi or a boat journey, and I had no real idea of the geography. I didn't know where he was.

I, who had never left him and never would, didn't know where he was.

Silvia was still talking. She was exhausted and needed a break for a day or two. She was coming home tomorrow and she'd tell me more then. She'd see me at around 10am. Meantime, Mr Smith would be cared for by Manola and the other women on site, and the *maestros* were still on hand to monitor him. He would be fine.

I think I asked her how he could be both fine and critical. I think she said he wasn't in immediate danger. I don't remember the details, but I do remember she contradicted herself enough to allow me to disbelieve her and to strengthen my resolve to make my way to him somehow.

Of course he wasn't dying. He needed to go right to the edge for his body to be cleared of the toxic invasion in his belly. There was a parallel here with the chemotherapy that he'd declined at home – when it works, it works by destroying indiscriminately, leaving the body weakened before it can be built up again. He'd known this would happen. He would reach a turning point very soon.

I knew that, but the fear knew something else, something that this 'I' of mine couldn't agree to. My 'I' didn't know what to do when the call ended, so she paced the floor again. Eventually, she turned towards home, via social media.

For much of my adult life I'd played the role of soother, nurturer, reassurer, and the habit was ingrained. I couldn't tell people how I felt in this moment – I didn't know how I felt, for one thing, and for another, I needed them to share in my stubborn optimism. I needed them not to worry. If they worried for us, the optimism might lose its grip, and it was all I had in this moment. I needed to spread it so it could grow.

I don't remember how those conversations went but there were quite a few of them, and now, when I remember that day, I feel the gratitude that might have gone unexpressed in the moment. People at home were six hours ahead and they had beds to go to, but they stayed with me. The soother needed soothing, and for the first time in over thirteen years, Mr Smith wasn't at hand to do the job.

I don't believe I slept. In the morning I turned to my crystal pendant for reassurance. I'd been dabbling in pendulum dowsing for some time, and was never certain of how or whether it worked, but I needed to do something; needed to *know* somehow. 'Is he still alive this morning?' A wide, slow, clockwise circle traced through the air in response. That looked like a pretty definitive yes, but could I trust it, or was the churning in my gut a more reliable guide? In truth, I could hear no guidance, and I had no idea what any of it meant.

10am came and went. I paced, I sat, I paced some more. I changed my mind. I wouldn't go to him: how could I risk his life like that? I changed it back again: how could I let him go through this on his own?

Hours passed in the nausea and heat of this daylight hell. Somehow, I lived through it and when the subtly altered form of Silvia appeared in the doorway in the late afternoon, it was terror and not relief that she brought with her.

I couldn't face it, but here it was, face to face. I couldn't look into her face, but I had to. And when I did, there was no bad news in it, no horror. Relief could be allowed in now, for a while.

There was no news of any kind, really. She had nothing to add to what she'd already told me. It was now Tuesday and the original plan had been for Mr Smith to return before the end of the week, but changes of plan were commonplace. There was another new plan, just as pliable, and affordable. By now money was the furthest thing from my mind but in the world Silvia still inhabited, it remained crucial, and her solution had budget in mind.

The *maestros* would be away for six weeks. Ambrosio had already left to work in the Sacred Valley, and Tobias and Eduardo were due in Russia on Friday. Meantime, Mr Smith was receiving intensive treatments from them both, and Silvia needed me to go into town and withdraw more cash to pay them. In their absence, Manola's sister Sofia and her young husband Jaime would take over. Sofia was a *vegitalista,* intimately involved in plant lore with extensive knowledge of medicinal uses and *dietas,* and although Jaime had only five years' experience as a shaman behind him, he was more than able to support Mr Smith till the elders came back in early August. We'd pay Sofia on a day-to-day basis and Jaime per ceremony. We hadn't anticipated the extra spending but Silvia had negotiated favourable terms for us.

I tried to take all this in but the insistent call of the elephant in the room drowned it out. I couldn't ignore it any longer; I had to ask the question. Was Mr Smith expected to come through this?

A few weeks earlier, Silvia had told us about the Shipibo's use of poisonous plants to euthanise their dying, and I'd implored her to let us know if ever this was being considered for Mr Smith. I believed in no such possibility, of course, but in the hypothetical scenario, I'd need to be able to take him home while he was still well enough to travel. She'd assured me that it just wouldn't happen. The Shipibo were mindful of other cultural sensibilities, to say nothing of the legal repercussions, and they reserved such methods for their own people. In any case, we were here to get Mr Smith well and we were not going to entertain any notions to the contrary.

Now that she *was* entertaining such a notion she had no answer to my question, but there was something she wanted me to know about the Shipibo: they never gave up hope. You were always going to get better, in their view – until you didn't. They would keep trying, and believing, until the very end. She had a suggestion to make: She wanted Mr Smith to write a 'legal document' absolving me of responsibility in the event of his death. Otherwise, I might end up in prison.

I wasn't sure of how Peruvian law worked but I did know that ayahuasca has legal status in South America, so I couldn't make sense of this. One of Silvia's favourite anecdotes was of the time when she was very sick and thought she was dying, and when she'd offered to do the same for Tobias, he'd laughed. He and

Manola had laughed off the notion that Mr Smith might die, too, when we'd told them of the prognosis from home. I wondered whether he'd still be laughing now. I wondered whether he'd even said what Silvia claimed he had.

Without clear information, I had no basis for any belief or any course of action. I was never sure whether to believe Silvia about anything anymore – was that even true about the euthanasia treatment? Were we in breach of the law somehow? And if it was true that the Shipibo never gave up, how could I have any confidence in their assurances that he'd be okay?

I had hoped for news that his condition had improved since yesterday. I had hoped that a talk with Silvia might help to guide my next steps, but he was no better and still I had no idea of what to do.

Silvia did though. She'd had time on the boat to think, and she thought I should go to him. Tobias had no right to keep us apart.

That was something else I'd hoped for – her compliance, as someone who'd seen him only this morning, with my impulse to be with him. What about Tobias, though? His opinion surely carried more weight, and he'd said no. This was Mr Smith's unique and precious life. I couldn't do anything to risk it but I couldn't be absent at its end.

Silvia was arranging for a boat to take her back tomorrow, and I could be on it if I chose.

In the end, the spirit of ayahuasca helped me clear my path through the confusion. Horacio was due to arrive after dark, and by morning, I was in no doubt. I was going.

Silvia had decided to treat herself to a night in the hotel before returning to the jungle, and we arranged to meet at the port in the early afternoon. I packed a few things and Emilio loaded them onto the back of his mototaxi for me. This was another day in which Mr Smith's condition could change for better or worse, and still I didn't know. I didn't know how Tobias would react to my arrival, or what life in the jungle would be like. All I knew was this: once I got there, Mr Smith and I would never be separated again.

I've been known to take a long time over decisions, becoming immobilised in deliberation and finally breaking through, my intuition supplying the momentum to facilitate, and *necessitate*, action. Now here I was, moving, through the wide hot streets with breeze in my hair and grit in my eyes. I was doing something, and the doing made everything just a little bit better.

I was doing something – until Emilio's phone rang and he pulled over. I knew before he answered it that it was Silvia calling. She had decided to wait another day. Caring for Mr Smith had taken a heavy toll on her and she didn't feel well enough to travel. She'd persuaded the man she'd spent the night with, a casual romantic interest called Roberto, to come with us. She'd feel safer with a man around, since for at least the first week after the *maestros'* departure, Jaime wouldn't be able to join us and there would just be us and Sofia in the camp. Tobias had promised to call with an update on Mr Smith's condition later today, and meantime, Emilio could go down to the port and use his bartering skills to secure us a more reliable private boat for tomorrow.

She tried to reassure me that Mr Smith could wait another day, but I was plunged again into stagnation and trepidation. I couldn't move now – I couldn't do anything – and another day might be a day too late. Tobias didn't call.

I forget who it was that suggested inviting Horacio to conduct a ceremony that night, and I was surprised at my own assent, but this time, we were drinking for Mr Smith. This ceremony was conducted in the same way as any other of Horacio's offerings: simple icaros, smoke and copious applications of *Agua de Florida* to counter the nauseous upsurgings. But that night's libations were received with newly emergent urgency and passion that brought Mr Smith, all those hours away, back into my presence.

Mamma Aya's message was clear this time, and of course I knew it; I always had known it. He was, and always would be, just fine. Just as he'd told me himself, that Sunday afternoon in the German hotel room. He was more than fine, and I could rejoice in the knowing of it.

I spent much of the night in laughter and song, and by the time Emilio and I stopped by the hotel to pick up Silvia and Roberto, I was sleepless but buoyant in anticipation of seeing my love again.

8

Reunion

June – July 2014

It was a better boat, big enough to take the three of us and Roberto's dog in comfort. It had a powerful motor so it would be much faster and too imposing for the pirates to tackle. We were as safe as we could be, and with last night's lesson learned, I had no reason to fear. Now and again, Silvia interrupted my contemplation of the broad waterway and the dense green shoreline. Wasn't I scared of pirates? Wasn't I scared of piranhas? Only last week Ambrosio had killed an anaconda in self-defence – wasn't I scared of being in the jungle?

I wasn't. I wasn't scared of anything anymore. Mr Smith was okay. His spirit had told me so more than once, and my trust in that was blossoming in proportion to the waning of my interest in Silvia's opinions. Her stories seemed less and less relevant to me now, as I enjoyed the soft rippling of the surface water. After the oppression of near-confinement by the lagoon, everything felt new and fresh. Pucallpa was colourful in a cheaply commercial way; this was a different kind of colour, a lustrous gift of nature. Time and space loosened their grip as I claimed my freedom in the company of the waterfowl that alighted momentarily on the riverbank.

The rural scene at the journey's end revealed a new level of quaintness. The straggle of mototaxis along the narrow dirt road looked familiar enough, and so did the drivers competing for our business, but the buildings were small and sparse and the natural landscape had retained its sovereignty here. As we rounded the corner away from the bank, we stopped abruptly outside a simple hut, and a girl of around eight or nine emerged carrying a metal canister. By now, novelty was unremarkable, and I didn't bother to wonder why – all would be revealed, or not; it didn't matter either way. Still, I found it delightful when she poured the contents into the fuel tank and took a few coins from the driver, and I stored her away as an anecdote to charm Mr Smith. There was going to be so much to talk about.

But that depended on how he was, and my too-human heart began to lurch again as we approached our final destination. We came to a sudden halt in what looked like nowhere; beyond this narrow dirt track, the driver didn't know the way. We would have to walk from here, and as we stepped down, we found ourselves surrounded by a throng of children. Here were the progeny of Manola's and Tobias' extended family, pouring out from tiny wooden huts to walk alongside us.

Partway along the path through the trees, I realised that one of these small people was not a child at all. Sofia, Manola's sister, greeted me with a gentle smile and a stroke of my arm. Mr Smith was better today, she said. He'd had a breakthrough. He'd been given sacred plant offerings reserved only for healers, which conferred on him the power to heal as well as to be healed. So my message from last night had been accurate; all was well.

I cried, and laughed, and cried again. Relief, elation, feelings I couldn't name. Further along the path, Manola appeared, and we hugged and wept and laughed together. Further still, Tobias, calling my name joyfully and thrusting his arms wide to receive me. This was the man who'd forbidden me to come? This was the man who showed me the most enthusiastic welcome I'd ever experienced.

He was so happy I was here, he said. More tears, more laughter, more hugs. He slapped his hand to my shoulder and guided me to the hub of the camp, a sturdy wooden structure where, through the large mesh window, I could just see the top of the dear, cherished, familiar head of Mr Smith.

He was thin, yes, but I didn't see that. All I saw was Mr Smith.

And I kissed his face and tasted his tears and felt his heartbeat, and he was still beautiful.

And I saw nothing else, and I felt nothing else, and there was nothing else.

He stood up to meet me, and I eased him back into his hammock while we kissed and wept and talked away the interminable two weeks we'd just miraculously navigated.

Yesterday he'd watched the cat, starving and skinny, kill a rat for her only kitten, and he'd been touched by the selflessness of the act. The kitten had been given to a visiting family just a few hours later. He didn't know who they were; there were so many comings and goings. There had been the young German who had been so companionable; the daughter of friends from the USA; members of the extended family. The ceremonies were so much more powerful here, with three *maestros* working harmoniously together. He was not surprised that people were willing to travel for many days to reach them. They never advertised, but somehow, those who needed them could always find them. His gratitude was immeasurable. He hadn't missed Silvia but he'd been looking forward to her return because he'd almost dared to hope that she'd bring me with her.

There had never been a time when he'd felt his condition to be critical. He'd been weakened, yes, and he'd felt horrible, but he was better now, and the pain was reducing.

Later, as he slept, the women and children chased bats from the dormitory hut and exchanged his single bed for a double. His room – now our room – was basic but comfortable. I wondered, why the big deal about my not being able to cope with life here? Sure, access to electricity and running water was sparse and there was no flush toilet, but the living conditions were no more basic than at the lagoon. Mr Smith told me later that he'd asked himself the same questions and wondered why I hadn't been invited in the first place.

We sat in ceremony that night, in the purpose-built *maloca*, and I had my first taste of the authentic jungle experience. It felt like a celebration; the room was full of family members to whom I was yet to be introduced. They included children of all ages, including Sofia's nursing infant. Their chattering babble subsided as the candles were extinguished, and again we drank in silence until the singing began. This time, I was encouraged to lie next to Mr Smith, and when it was over, we slipped into our double bed. By now, he was too skinny and sore to hold close, so I held his hand through the night, and we made it enough.

Manola woke us in the early morning, and in a flurry of fleeting embraces, our healers were gone. Not long after that, Roberto left too, after some sort of lovers' tiff. We weren't disappointed; his and Silvia's combined energies provided no comfort. After he'd gone, and with Sofia and the children appearing for just a few minutes each day, we found ourselves again in intimacy with Silvia, and at times her manic side slipped out of sight for a while.

The evenings were long and dark, and we each swung in our hammocks, conversing about spiritual journeys, healing, love and life. Mr Smith's star shone softly in the candlelight on these nights. I could almost feel him back home in the pub with friends, in gentle discourse, exchanging ideas with typical modesty and generosity. Back in the dorm hut, Silvia confessed she'd begun to see a strength in me she hadn't seen before. Was it newly acquired, she wondered? Or had it always been there, unnoticed? I told her she'd have to ask Mr Smith.

Life became simpler. We had candles and torches to light our way in the evenings; I could draw water from the well; and soon we abandoned the long-drop composting toilet in favour of a simple bucket, cleaning it out each time with Agua de Florida, the most abundant and useful of resources.

After a few days, Jaime returned and the ceremonies resumed. Jaime's youthful appearance belied his wisdom and power, and his ceremonies were sweetly nurturing. We continued to lie on our mats hand-in-hand on these nights – Silvia had forbidden this, but Jaime knew the healing energy of a loving touch, and he encouraged it. In the mornings I paid him, vaguely mindful that the cash would run out sooner or later but with a curious confidence that things would work out.

The days drifted by, more or less peacefully. Sofia and Jaime came each day to make the special soup that formed Mr Smith's *dieta,* and to sing to him while beating a large bunch of leaves rhythmically onto his flesh, until the leaves were limp and the medicine had penetrated his skin. It didn't hurt, even when the medicine came in the form of giant stinging nettles. He was moving beyond pain now.

Time began to stretch. Days seemed endless, so much life was in them, and life flowed slowly, in natural rhythm. Animals were part of our small soulful community. As well as the hungry cat and several scrawny dogs, there were chickens scratching in the grass around the buildings, wild boar wandering through the camp and a herd of cattle passing by on occasion. A hummingbird began to visit our window each morning. Dragonflies and tarantulas shared our space, and Mr Smith urged me to appreciate them and not be afraid. We were in their territory, and they were gracious in allowing our presence, harmlessly.

One afternoon, through the window I saw a boy with a rucksack approaching the door. This was Simon, the young German, returning from his adventures, and Silvia and Mr Smith greeted him like the dear friend he'd become in their few days together. His limbs bore the faded remains of the same violent, red, oozing and agonising sores that had begun to colonise my skin via the mosquito bites, and he had allowed the medicines, and the plant spirits, and his body, to cleanse him. Here was a kindred spirit, who played guitar and shared songs and stories. We didn't share food with him though. He ate at the home of

Manola's uncle, along the path from the centre.

We didn't share food but we did share ceremony, and we began to wonder about the financial arrangements. Silvia told us that Simon's parents had paid a lot of money for a complete package with the family – one she'd hinted that we couldn't afford.

A few days after Simon's arrival, Silvia announced that she was taking another break. Ambrosio was due to return from Cusco for a few days, and he would be accompanied by someone Silvia didn't want to be around. It took some probing on my part to understand who and why, but eventually she explained that Louise was a Canadian who'd married into the extended family and who had a close connection with them. Silvia didn't like her, and neither would we. She was trouble and we were to avoid her as best we could.

Silvia left; she would be back. Ambrosio and his wife Marcela arrived, with Louise, her young daughter and their friend. As it turned out, Louise was friendly, interested, intelligent and knowledgeable, and we both warmed to her quickly. On the first morning after their arrival, I left Mr Smith asleep and went to the main building to make myself some breakfast. The kitchen, which had been silent till now, was buzzing with life and an abundant breakfast was being served. I was offered a plate: I declined. This was a financial issue – the deal was that I was strictly self-catering.

Louise was visibly perturbed by this, and she explained how things worked around here. We're family, she said, whether your stay lasts a week or a lifetime. We eat together; we share. I explained about our ad hoc arrangement, and she suggested talking to Ambrosio.

We had wondered about our payment plan: would we be asked for double the fees now that Ambrosio was joining Jaime in ceremony? It was important to pay our way but there had been so many unexpected expenses and this wasn't foreseen. The ceremonies were all the richer, though, for Ambrosio's presence, and again, we fell back on trust that everything would work out.

Meanwhile, Silvia, banished by her own discomfort, had asked for regular progress reports. On occasion, Simon and I went to the village with Manola's brother Alonso, to pick up supplies from the shop and to keep in touch with home at the internet café. On the day of Louise's arrival, I called Silvia to say Mr Smith was gaining strength. She said it was time to begin building up his diet; I was to put some semolina in his soup and report back in a couple of days.

During that night's ceremony, Mr Smith lay on his mat writhing in agony. As Ambrosio ministered to him, Louise quietly asked whether we'd strayed from his protocol in any way. A groan arose among the family when I said what I'd done. Why did I do that? He was on a very particular diet, one that must be adhered to. Thankfully, Ambrosio was able to help him through it, but for a while he had been in some danger.

Louise's approach was gentle: everyone appreciated Silvia's big heart, but we were to be careful of acting on advice from anyone other than the healers themselves. By the end of the conversation, there was clarity on all sides. Silvia was not apprenticed to Tobias, as she'd told us. She'd come to be healed and had claimed an association with the family ever since, but she had no expertise, and had not been acting under Tobias' supervision. By the time Mr Smith and I were able to discuss all of this the following day, we'd reached the same conclusion.

Our shared ambivalence towards Silvia had been veering more towards distrust, but there was compassion for her, too, as her vulnerability showed itself. One evening, she'd complained to me, forlornly, that she'd helped a lot of people but that nobody wanted to know her now. I confided this to Mr Smith and we sorrowed in her obvious torment, even as we began to understand why.

Louise's ability to interpret bridged the language gap, and

Ambrosio was receptive to our enquiries. He estimated that Mr Smith would be ready to go home in October. It was a nonsense to insist, or even suggest, that we should return here. The shamans understood that, just as they were indigenous to this place, we were indigenous to ours. We belonged back at home and we'd go back fully healed and ready to reintegrate into the life that was ours. The arrangement Silvia had brokered for us hadn't been comfortable for them; paying individuals caused imbalance within the family. They'd prefer us to pay a flat fee, one that would be evenly distributed, and to share in family life and in the healing they could offer as a team.

By the end of the afternoon, we were enlightened; we hadn't realised what a heavy load we'd been carrying till we put it down. An arrangement was in place that left us enough in the bank to make our way home and pay the rent when we got there, and we had an end in sight. We also had an apology: we should never have been exposed to so many healers with their different and potentially conflicting treatments. This was hardly Ambrosio's responsibility but he was sorry it had happened in his country.

It hardly mattered now – Silvia may not be the healer she'd claimed to be but she'd brought us here, where real healing could take place. Gradually, our new family became familiar and cherished. Ramira, a tender-hearted aunt of the family in traditional Shipibo dress, did the laundry and supported her husband Ruben, the *vegetalisto* who administered the catahua bark that allowed Mr Smith's body to cleanse so potently. Alonso swept floors and drove the truck and the mototaxi; his wife Exilda helped in the kitchen. Everyone had equal status; all work, and all people, were valued.

There was just one task to get out of the way now, and I wasn't looking forward to it. Alonso drove me to the village, with Simon to hold my hand; Silvia was unpredictable and I felt delicate. I took a deep breath and tapped in her number. Mr Smith was doing well; we were forever grateful to her for bringing us here; we were in good hands and we knew that she needed a good long break after everything she'd done for us.

She took it well, on this occasion, and we relaxed into those good hands for a while.

9

Letting Go

July 2014

It was around this time, I think, that our connection became perfect. In an exquisite dance yielding to his necessary transformation, Mr Smith held out his hand to me in invitation. His body knew what to do, and so did I. As we fell into step, all our wounds and irrelevances slipped away and were purged. All that remained were the pure, ever-present core of our merged souls and two physical beings, one of them spent.

His body cleansed and weakened, and, as promised, the Shipibo never gave up on him. Ambrosio, Louise and their party stayed only a few days before moving on to Canada, but the other *maestros* were due back on August 1st, our wedding anniversary. This year, there would be no champagne, no restaurant meal, not even a card, but we would celebrate anyway. All that Mr Smith was drinking now was cinnamon tea, and we would make do with that. On my occasional trips to the village, I bought all the cinnamon sticks in the shop to make his infusion under Jaime's instruction. I made his tea, washed our clothes and aired the mattress on the floor beside his hammock that served as a treatment station. The family ministered to him with herbal baths, steam treatments and poultices, and I wrapped him in bandages, towels, blankets and love.

I sang to him as I rocked him, and once again, songs appeared as we needed them. There had been one I'd known from our shamanic adventures back home, and both its melody and its words had eluded me. One night, as the ceremony closed, it arrived fully in my mind, and I began to sing it to him. It was lilting and gentle, and although I can't be certain, my voice seemed to hold a new and unexpected sweetness as I sang:

You are forever pure; you are forever true
And the dream of this world can never touch you
So give up your attachments; give up your confusion
And fly to the space that's beyond all illusion
Suddhosi Buddhosi, Vedic lullaby

Once, mid-verse, I stopped singing.

'Oh, this is a lullaby! Is it okay to sing you a lullaby as I rock you?'

It was okay. His smile was radiant; he'd heard the invitation and he was ready.

I was drinking less and less ayahuasca. Mr Smith's healing was still the focus of the ceremonies and he was still receiving songs and preparations throughout the nights, but his body was too weak to drink, and he no longer needed to. I didn't need it either anymore; the spirit of the vine had imparted all the gifts she had for us. I continued to take *un poquito* – just a little – sometimes, to stay attuned, but the work was done. My only job now was to attend to Mr Smith, and so on those nights, I lay with him in silence.

Now that we were always together, the part of me that forgot not to be fearful didn't notice the rapid change in his body. He was no longer able to walk to the shower huts for his daily herbal baths, so we developed a new method whereby he crouched on the wooden floor while I poured cups of leafy water over him. One of my early morning tasks was to sweep up yesterday's leaves before laying out his mattress ready for Ruben to bring the catahua. One afternoon, while I was patting his still-perfect torso dry, he stopped me and drew me into his arms.

'I promised I wouldn't leave you, didn't I? If I do, I'm sorry.'

The part of me that forgot I was fearless couldn't receive this. All I could say was, 'But you're not going to... you're getting better.'

And then, from the wiser part of me, 'And even if you do go, you won't ever leave me, really, will you?'

Of course he wouldn't. He wouldn't, not ever.

We stopped attending ceremony a few days later. The *maloca* was reached by several steps and he was finding it more and more difficult to climb them. At the end of one ceremony it took three men to support him down to the ground, across the short distance to the dorm hut and up the few steps to our room. I trailed behind, carrying the cushions and blankets and the torch to see us safely back. It was slow and I was scared – of deadly snakes in the dark and of the sight of this figure whose frailty was so at odds with the Mr Smith I knew. The Shipibo are characteristically compactly built, and he looked tall and agonisingly spare in contrast. As I helped him into bed that night, lifting his legs onto the mattress, he apologised again. He was sorry I had to see him like this. I told him I'd never seen him so perfect.

We stayed in our room after that. Jaime was still conducting ceremonies for Simon and the family, and his icaros drifted into our little space. At the end of each ceremony, he came to our room to sing and administer to us both. In the mornings we were visited by our friend the hummingbird, and each day, I crossed the ground to the kitchen to collect Mr Smith's soup, picking my way over rushing paths of ants. Alonso tended to my open sores and taught me how to tap the trees behind the common room for the rich red *sangre de grada*, the sap that I needed to treat them with. I never stayed away for long; back in our room, I'd swing in the hammock, face-to-face with Mr Smith on the bed. We talked, but not much; there was little need for words now.

We still owed the family some money; it was due in cash, at a time when I could get back to Pucallpa. I'd need to stay there for two nights, to withdraw my daily limit on three days, and I planned to go as soon as Mr Smith was strong enough for me to leave him. Our cash supplies were very low now. There had been occasional visits from a nurse from the village who'd been administering a sodium drip, and there was just enough in my purse to cover the next anticipated visit in a few days' time.

Simon came to our room one early morning, and, since we'd all been living on little more than corn spaghetti for the previous few days, I knew what he was going to say. There was no food, and no money to buy any. We needed to talk about what to do.

I was torn. Our contribution was required to feed us all, but to get access to it would mean going away for two days, and Mr Smith had never needed me more. A few days earlier, Simon and I had found him slumped on the floor after he'd tried to get out of bed by himself. He needed close personal care now, as well as his daily treatments from the family. Simon offered to step in. Back home, he'd volunteered in residential care centres, and he was unfazed. He'd witnessed Mr Smith's weakness and was willing to help. He was part of this family too.

We were reluctant but it was necessary. I handed over the contents of my purse and Alonso bought some food in the village to tide us over. A few days later, on a Tuesday, Alonso and I were on a boat again.

I got the money, and I got another task out of the way too. On the day before we set off, Simon was going to the village. I didn't want to go with him – I had to make the most of my time with Mr Smith, and anyway there was no need since I'd be able to get online in Pucallpa. I asked him how he'd feel about calling Silvia for me. Our luggage, visas and passports were still in her house, and she'd left some of her things in the room opposite ours. But Simon didn't want to speak to her, and we couldn't blame him, so I went to the village after all, and composed what I hoped was an amicable message on social media, letting her know I'd be in town and would call in to collect our stuff. I still had a key, so she didn't have to wait in. Secretly, I hoped she wouldn't be there.

She wasn't. As we approached the house, Roberto cycled past us in the opposite direction. He waved to us; it looked like he'd just been for a visit. We reached the house to find the door locked, and momentarily, I was relieved. Then Alonso noticed the padlock.

We could hear Roberto's dog inside, so we reasoned that someone would be back soon. We waited a while, then we asked the neighbour who ran the little soda stall just beneath the house whether she knew where Silvia was. She had left, she told us conspiratorially, delighting in the gossip, and nobody knew where she was. Roberto lived here now, alone with his dog. He should be back soon.

We waited almost three hours before Alonso resorted to breaking the padlock. The scene inside was violent. The filthy old toilet from the back porch was now in the middle of the ceremony room; the kitchen sink had been ripped out; there was debris everywhere and our stuff was strewn all over the place. My laptop (Silvia had advised against taking it on the boat for fear it would attract pirates) was stashed behind a cabinet in Silvia's room and my iPad, my shoes and some of my prettiest clothes were nowhere to be seen. Our suitcases were infested with nimble cockroaches and everything was covered in a film of dust. Our passports were there though, and our visas. Once we were sure of those, we got out of there fast, and hailed a mototaxi back to town.

The hotel owner, a European expat, was concerned about the open wounds on my legs and arms, more for my sake than for the bloodstains on his sheets. Alonso knew though: this was a necessary cleansing reaction that he'd seen many times; it would stop as soon as I left the sacred energy of the jungle. Next day, I stayed in the hotel and took advantage of the Wi-Fi to connect again with loved ones at home and to buy some music for Mr Smith to cherish. Alonso was staying at a family home in another part of town, but he visited me, walked with me to the bank and helped me clear the cockroaches out of our luggage. I could live with ants and spiders but cockroaches unnerved me.

On the third day we withdrew more cash and went home, with an impressive supply of food that Alonso somehow managed to carry down the steep embankment and onto the public transport boat that also functioned as a cargo vessel for every community along the riverbank. Livestock, motorbikes, furniture and four-generation families were crammed together, with garish hammocks strung above the benches to accommodate even more people. Remembering the discomfort of the outbound trip, I bought a cheap one from one of the pedlars on board and tried to sleep the six hours away.

We went home. Home, for me, was where Mr Smith was, and I found him in bed where I'd left him. The family had rallied round; Simon had barely left his side and Ramira had slept in the hammock by the bed. Jaime had moved into the room opposite ours at around the time we'd stopped attending ceremony, to provide on-call care. There had been attentive and loving support throughout my absence; still, the wearily rapturous smile said he was glad I was back.

It was Thursday afternoon when I returned to him. It didn't matter what day it was; the routine was the same. But every morning, as I descended the wooden steps of the dorm building and stepped into the sunlight, I thought of the progression of days marked by the calendar on the wall in the main hut. We were treading water now, waiting for the return of the medicine men. The purging had become lighter; the cleansing was almost complete and soon it would be August. Meantime, with my smartphone fully charged, I had the gift of music to offer him. I would download more on my next visit to town, in a few weeks' time. That could be anticipated with some excitement, since he'd be so much stronger by then. For now, here was Mr Cohen again.

We played the album so often that now, when I think of any act I performed in our little wooden room, the soundtrack forms the biggest part of the memory. Often, we pressed 'repeat' before it ended, so that the first track became the most familiar:

Going home without my sorrow
Going home sometime tomorrow
Going home to where it's better than before
Going home without my burden
Going home behind the curtain
Going home without this costume that I wore.
From *Going Home,* written by Leonard Cohen.

My stubborn, fearful mind resisted still, but we knew. Sometime tomorrow.

10

Completion

Sunday July 20th 2014

There was no pain anymore. There hadn't been for a while, but the discomfort had been increasing. So much of his flesh and muscle had dissolved now that no matter how he lay, there was no ease in any position for long. He had no strength to manipulate his frame, so he relied on me to lift him and arrange his unfamiliar limbs.

It had been a long and sleepless night of apologetic requests for help to change position. In the feeble early light, he asked again. I knelt up, shuffled my arms round his shoulders and eased him upwards; in moments like this we paused a few seconds to reclaim, briefly, the old intimacy that had so recently been ours. I arranged his pillows and laid him gently down. As I lay back I could just see, on the outside of the window facing the bed, a large butterfly, wings spread, motionless, facing down. On the wall next to the window was a spider – a big one, a tarantula; it, too, was still. These were our totems for today, and I knew why they'd come. Haunted, I closed my eyes, just for a moment.

Suddenly I was winded. He'd tried to sit up and had fallen over onto my chest. Neither of us could move. I chastised him, gently, for not asking for help and, as softly as I could, called for Jaime, who came cheerfully and left again to fetch another of the men to help lift him. In those few minutes I felt Mr Smith's warmth, the life in him; and the butterfly and the spider remained, untroubled.

As the men pulled him up, he cried out in momentary confusion. Jaime began to sing to him, while I lay one hand on his brow and the other on his heart, whispering consolation. His body flopped forwards. A hushful moan emerged from his lips and the deep blue eyes softened, then dimmed.

For a fraction of a second I thought of begging Jaime to bring him back, but in the moment the thought arrived, I let it go. Mr Smith was no longer there; he wasn't coming back. This sore and skinny body was no longer fit for purpose, and even if a miracle could be arranged, I couldn't ask him to occupy it again. He'd finished with it, and now he was going home.

And as I held the precious bones of him and spoke to his sweet face, telling soft secrets, a glittering thread appeared between him, at home, and my tiny, shaking form there in the room. This was the thread that bound us, and it set us free.

It set him free of his burden, and it set me free of my fear. All of his human strength pulsed through that thread and found a new home in my being. A weightless mass permeated my cells, and I knew I could go on. In those last moments my body had begun to signal a purge, and, reluctantly, urgently, I left the room three times in that timeless span while he lay silent on the bed. His presence was magnified now; it filled the room, and the building, and everything outside of it. Purified, I lay within it, kissing his head, stroking his feet and softly, softly whispering.

The family flooded the room and the children were chattering outside and peering through the windows. One of the women was screaming his name, over and over. I wanted to scream back, to make her stop – but Mr Smith needed me to be calm, and I was. I asked to be alone with him, and in the sudden quiet I held him till his lips were pale. They would be cold now; there was no last kiss in them. Slowly, I eased his blanket over his head.

There followed an eventful week. I could tell you about the suffering and the anguish; the acts of kindness and the acts that felt cruel to me, the receiver. I only mention them, some of them, to offer a taste of Mr Smith's continued presence throughout it all.

He was there as I lay holding his motionless, covered body on the back of the truck. He was there on the boat, when the dolphin surged alongside us and splashed a greeting. He was there in the warmth of the sun on my back as I stroked the blankets, not daring now to look beneath them.

He was there in the moment when, leaving the morgue that night in the dark heat, I felt my hand strangely empty with no one to hold it. Instantly, wordlessly, Alonso took my left hand and Simon my right, and I knew that the comfort came from him as much as from them.

He was there in the moment when they offered me the option of cremation rather than the added nightmare and unmeetable expense of transporting his body home. I experienced him as clearly as when my senses had seen and touched and heard him in life. I felt him tell me, 'I don't need this body anymore, but I do need you to look after yourself and take the route that's easiest for you.' It was characteristically good advice, offered with devotion, to steer me towards self-care as a new habit now that life had changed.

He was there in the moments when, in the hotel in Lima, the pain-fuelled messages reached my social media pages: personal attacks from the friend and the sister who couldn't understand our choices, couldn't accept the news and found me worthy of blame; and from Silvia, re-emerging panic-stricken and abusive. He helped me see beyond the acts to the distress behind them, and to find compassion in those moments.

I would love to say I felt him influence the global Team Smith to care for me in the many ways that they did, but I have a feeling that they did those things all by themselves. Still, I have no doubt that he appreciated and delighted in their friendship as he always had. I'm sure he helped the key players to arrange for the memorial service to take place on our anniversary, a day that was always going to be worthy of celebration.

He was there throughout everything that happened in that

week, but those things are not in themselves part of our story; they have nothing to do with the happy ending. Our happy ending is unexpected; it's not the one we hoped for. It's not tied in a wedding-posy bow. Real life, as we know, is never that neat.

Real life, at its conclusion, can be held with courage and grace. I've seen that. I've learned that, sometimes, our healing reaches beyond the physical, and is complete even as the body decays. I've learned that for our lives to be complete, we need to stop striving to keep them; we need to let them go, in the time when they must. I learned that when we can see the glittering thread, there's nothing more to strive for. I learned all of that from observing Mr Smith. Those observations are part of the particular kind of happiness that we found, the two of us, at the end of our story.

The happy ending lies in Mr Smith finding peace and keeping me safe through all the drama. It lies in promises kept and in perfection, not attained but revealed. It lies in the discovery that our happy ending was there at the beginning; it was woven into every moment we were together and every moment we were joyful in anticipation of being together. It glittered in every moment we knew we were loved. Actually, now that I look back, I don't see a beginning: I don't remember a time when we didn't have what we now know we have. There are no beginnings in eternity.

There are no endings either, in truth. Endings are really just pauses. The most we can say is that this is the end of a part of a story. It's the end of the part where Mr Smith teaches me that life is precious and perfect in its struggles and challenges; where he shows me that life is brief but love is infinite; it's the part where I learn through my fear that there's nothing to fear. And in the midst of the grief and longing that have shadowed my days, it is that learning that makes this the happiest possible ending of this part of the story of me and Mr Smith.

Epilogue

Monday July 28th 2014
9.45pm
Glasgow, Scotland

It's been a long day. I arrived at the airport in Lima earlier than was necessary, because of that need I have, to be in motion rather than stagnant and helpless in a hotel room. That was well over thirty hours ago, and although the airline stewards were kind and attentive and I managed to sleep, I'm stunned by fatigue.

The Peruvian funeral director gave me a soft woven bag to contain the wooden box I chose for Mr Smith, and I've clung to it throughout the journey. Now, clutching it tightly to my chest with one hand and wobbling the overloaded luggage trolley with the other, finally, I reach the gate. Beyond it, the world is different.

Our family and friends, delegates of Team Smith, are on the other side. It's as we always imagined, except that we're different and they are too. This place is different to the one we left behind, and they're different to how I remember them. They're differently real, dearly loved in a new way.

And they're comfortingly familiar. Everyone and everything is changed, but I am indigenous to this place, as the Shipibo are indigenous to theirs. I belong here, in this strange familiar place. I belong here, for now.

And on an unknown date sometime in the future, Mr Smith will call me, and I will take the path he has cleared for me, and I'll follow him home.

Acknowledgements

Team Smith, too numerous to name individually, have played a vital supporting role in the production of this book. I thank them for their understanding, their love and their belief in me no matter what. I suspect they're largely oblivious to the extent of my gratitude, which reaches beyond my ability to express it. Still, I trust that they recognise themselves and know that they are appreciated.

To the characters who populate these pages, I offer my sincere thanks for their part in our story. I'd particularly like to mention our jungle family, devoted custodians of ancient lands, gentle guardians of sacred plants, and honoured caregivers. We are forever bound together, throughout this life and beyond it.

To those who have taken the trouble to read early drafts and to share with me the benefit of their insights, I offer my heartfelt gratitude. They include Ross Allan, Helen Briggs, Mark Eccles, Jennifer Miller, Susan Ure Reid, Harriet Stack and Maggy Whitehouse.

To the team at John Hunt Publishing, I'd like to say thank you for all the guidance and support they've offered throughout the process.

To anyone who has spent their money, hard-earned or otherwise, on a copy of this book, or who has simply picked it up and invested time in reading it, I offer humble thanks in the hope that they find something in it to serve them.

And to Mr Smith, who agreed right from the beginning to co-author a book with me: Thank you, my love. You always did keep your promises.

BOOKS

O is a symbol of the world, of oneness and unity; this eye represents knowledge and insight. We publish titles on general spirituality and living a spiritual life. We aim to inform and help you on your own journey in this life.

Visit our website: http://www.o-books.com

Find us on Facebook:

https://www.facebook.com/OBooks

Follow us on Twitter: @obooks

If you have enjoyed this book, why not tell other readers by posting a review on your preferred booksite? Recent bestsellers from O-Books are:

Heart of Tantric Sex
Diana Richardson
Revealing Eastern secrets of deep love and intimacy to Western couples.
Paperback: 978-1-90381-637-0
e-book: 978-1-84694-637-0

Crystal Prescriptions
The A-Z guide to over 1,200 symptoms and their healing crystals
Judy Hall
The first in the popular series of four books, this handy little guide is packed as tight as a pill-bottle with crystal remedies for ailments.
Paperback: 978-1-90504-740-6
e-book: 978-1-84694-629-5

Take Me To Truth
Undoing the Ego
Nouk Sanchez, Tomas Vieira
The best-selling step-by-step book on shedding the Ego, using the teachings of *A Course In Miracles*.
Paperback: 978-1-84694-050-7
e-book: 978-1-84694-654-7

The 7 Myths about Love...Actually!
The journey from your HEAD to the HEART of your SOUL
Mike George
Smashes all the myths about LOVE
Paperback: 978-1-84694-288-4
e-book: 978-1-84694-682-0

The Holy Spirit's Interpretation of the New Testament
A course in Understanding and Acceptance
Regina Dawn Akers
Following on from the strength of *A Course in Miracles*, NTI teaches us how to experience the love and oneness of God.
Paperback: 978-1-84694-085-9
e-book: 978-1-78099-083-5

The Message of A Course In Miracles
A translation of the text in plain language
Elizabeth A. Cronkhite
A translation of *A Course in Miracles* into plain, everyday language for anyone seeking inner peace. The companion volume, *Practicing a Course In Miracles*, offers practical lessons and mentoring.
Paperback: 978-1-84694-319-5
e-book: 978-1-84694-642-4

Rising in Love
My Wild and Crazy Ride to Here and Now, with Amma, the Hugging Saint
Ram Das Batchelder
Rising in Love conveys an author's extraordinary journey of spiritual awakening with the Guru, Amma.
Paperback: 978-1-78279-687-9
e-book: 978-1-78279-686-2

Thinker's Guide to God
Peter Vardy
An introduction to key issues in the philosophy of religion.
Paperback: 978-1-90381-622-6

Your Simple Path
Find happiness in every step
Ian Tucker
A guide to helping us reconnect with what is really important in our lives.
Paperback: 978-1-78279-349-6
e-book: 978-1-78279-348-9

Find more titles and sign up to our readers' newsletter at http://www.johnhuntpublishing.com/mind-body-spirit

Follow us on Facebook at https://www.facebook.com/OBooks and Twitter at https://twitter.com/obooks.

Most titles are published in paperback and as an e-book. Paperbacks are available in physical bookshops. Both print and e-book editions are available online. Readers of e-books can click on the live links in the titles to order.